AF600164

THE CANONICAL OBLIGATION OF PREACHING IN PARISH CHURCHES

THE CATHOLIC UNIVERSITY OF AMERICA

Canon Law Studies

No. 291

THE CANONICAL OBLIGATION OF PREACHING IN PARISH CHURCHES

A HISTORICAL SYNOPSIS AND A COMMENTARY

By

REVEREND JOSEPH L. ALLGEIER, J. C. L.

Priest of the Archdiocese of Louisville

A DISSERTATION

Submitted to the Faculty of the School of Canon Law of the Catholic University of America in Partial Fulfillment of the Requirements for the Degree of

DOCTOR OF CANON LAW

THE CATHOLIC UNIVERSITY OF AMERICA PRESS
WASHINGTON, D. C.
1949

Nihil Obstat:

EDUARDUS G. ROELKER, S. T. D., J. C. D.

Censor Deputatus

Washingtonii, D. C., die 23 maii, 1949.

Imprimatur:

JOANNES A. FLOERSH, D. D.

Archiepiscopus Ludovicopolitanus

Ludovicopoli, die 26 maii, 1949

PRINTED IN THE UNITED STATE OF AMERICA

SLATER & GILROY — LOUISVILLE, KY.

aa

TO MY FATHER

AND IN

MEMORY OF MY MOTHER

TABLE OF CONTENTS

TABLE OF CONTENTS

FOREWORD

The obligation to preach was enjoined upon the Apostles by Christ Himself before He ascended into heaven: "Go ye into the whole world and preach the gospel to every creature" (Mark, XVI:15). The obligation is certainly a grave one, since it is particularly through preaching that the truths of the Catholic faith are made known to men for their salvation.

To consider the historical development of the law concerning this obligation to preach "the gospel to every creature," and to be better enabled to understand and interpret the present law of the Church which calls for the fulfillment of this obligation, are the purposes of this work.

The general legislation of the Church in the early centuries was rather meager. The obligation at that time was particularly incumbent on the bishop. He was to see that this obligation was fulfilled by himself or by others whom he had appointed for this purpose. The Council of Trent, however, placed the obligation of preaching directly on the pastors and on all who had the care of souls. It also specified the days on which this obligation was to be fulfilled. The legislation after the Council of Trent continued to confirm and uphold this Council's decrees.

The law as promulgated in the Code of Canon Law is very similar to that of the Council of Trent. It is hoped that a commentary on this law will be of some advantage to pastors who have the obligation of preaching.

The writer takes this occasion to express his appreciation to the Most Reverend John A. Floersh, Archbishop of Louisville, for the opportunity to pursue graduate studies in the School of Canon Law at the Catholic University of America. He particularly expresses his sincere gratitude to the members of the Faculty of the School of Canon Law for the encouragement and assistance which they rendered in the preparation of this work.

PART ONE

HISTORICAL SYNOPSIS

CHAPTER I

EARLY ECCLESIASTICAL LEGISLATION

ARTICLE 1. *Preliminary Remarks*

The Code of Canon Law treats the subject of preaching under the twentieth Title of the Third Book. The first two canons are introductory. They state: The obligation of preaching the word of God is incumbent upon the Roman Pontiff for the universal Church, the bishops for the dioceses. The bishops are obligated personally to fulfill this duty; however, besides pastors, they should appoint capable men to assist them in carrying out this obligation fruitfully.[1] No one may undertake the ministry of preaching unless he has been authorized by a legitimate ecclesiastical superior, either in that the latter specifically has shared the faculty with him or in that he has conferred an office which carries with it the duty of preaching.[2]

In the second chapter of the same Title, canon 1337 to canon 1348, the Code gives the legislation concerning sacred preaching. The specific purpose here is to consider the obligation of preaching as it is to be fulfilled in parish churches.

The term *praedicato* can be understood in a twofold sense: first, as something that is said before, that is, prior to that event, and thus it implies a prophecy; secondly, as something that is said before, that is, in the presence of someone, and thus it implies an exhortation. It is in the latter meaning that the term is to be understood here. The word "preach" has come into the English language from the Latin through the French.[3]

The term *concio* in the early Latin meant a meeting place or a convention. In the course of the centuries it came to mean the discourse held at or during a meeting. Hence today this word designates the sermon.[4]

---

1. Can. 1327.
2. Can. 1328.
3. *A New English Dictionary on Historical Principles* (ed. James A. H. Murray and H. Bradley, Oxford: The Clarendon Press, 1888-1928), s. v. *preach*.
4. *Op. cit.*, s. v. *concio*.

It must be remembered, too, that the word "parish" underwent a particular development in the succeeding centuries. The denotation of this word in early ecclesiastical terminology differed from the meaning it ultimately acquired in the present legislation.

As is evident from the *Acts of the Apostles*, it was after the days of Pentecost that the Apostles spread the gospel to the cities and the countries surrounding Palestine. The group of Christians in a city became known as the *parochia*, from which the English word parish was ultimately derived. In the early Church the parish was what is called today the diocese.[5] This fact is also evident from the wording employed in the early Councils of Ancyra (314), of Antioch (341), of Chalcedon (451), and of Agde (506), when they dealt with the obligation of preaching.[6]

In the Eastern Church, in addition to the principal cities, many rural areas were christianized early. These places too were called parishes.[7] There was a development of a parochial system in the Orient as early as the fourth century. This was particularly notable in Alexandria. In the West, Rome had parishes before any other city. Rome was divided into *tituli*, to which were assigned priests. Later the parish system developed in other cities of the West as the need demanded. Hence the development of the parish was more a local problem than a general one. It was however in the Council of Trent (1545-1563) that the parish received its true canonical status.[8]

Accordingly, in the sense in which the parish was understood throughout the centuries, the obligation of preaching in parish churches will be considered in this work.

---

5. Scherer, *Handbuch des Kirchenrechtes* (2 vols., Graz, 1886-1898), I, 554; Wernz, *Ius Decretalium* (2 ed., 6 vols., Romae et Prati, 1906-1913), Lib. III, tit. XXXV, n. 730, footnote.

6. Hefele-LeClercq, *Histoire des Conciles* (10 vols. in 19, Paris: Letouzey et Ane, 1907-1938), II, 658; 1000 (hereafter cited Hefele-LeClercq).

7. Scherer, *Handbuch des Kirchenrechtes, I, 628*; 641-643.

8. Connolly, *The Canonical Erection of Parishes,* The Catholic University of America Canon Law Studies, n. 114 (Washington, D. C.: The Catholic University of America, 1938), pp. 16-29; 39.

ARTICLE 2. *The Persons Obligated to Preach*

a. Bishops

Since the bishops are the immediate successors of the Apostles[9] to whom Christ had given the command, the canonical obligation of preaching is primarily incumbent upon them. That this obligation belongs to the episcopate is also evident from the consecratory ceremonies.[10]

The organizational development of the early Church was such that it favored the bishop's fulfillment of this urgent obligation in his own person. The Church had spread particularly in the larger cities. In such places the bishop was placed as the overseer. He surrounded himself with a college of priests and deacons, who were to aid him in the fulfillment of all his episcopal obligations. However, it was the bishop alone who celebrated Mass and preached to the people. From the fourth century onward the Church took root also in the rural sections. This rural growth in the Church's membership occurred especially in the East. Thus it became impracticable, nay even impossible, for the bishop to preach to all the faithful, as he had done in earlier times. Hence in the rural churches the bishop found it necessary to delegate this work to others.

Despite this fact it always remained the duty of the bishop to preach. Throughout the centuries, when some of the bishops lost sight of this grave obligation, the matter was called to their attention. The Council in Trullo (692), although not considered canonical in the West, insisted that bishops should preach, especially on Sundays.[11] The bishop, however, was allowed to preach solely in his own city. As a penalty for preaching publicly in another city he was to desist from acting as a bishop, and in consequence was to perform simply the functions of a priest.[12]

The Capitularies of Charlemagne (814) similarly stressed the obligation of the bishop to preach.[13] In the first Capitulary of Aachen (810)

9. Can. 329, § 1; Cf. Herve, *Manuale Theologiae Dagmaticae* (4 vols., Vol. I, 19. ed., Westminster, Md.: The Newman Bookshop, 1943), I, 375-377.

10. *Pontificale Romanum*: "Accipe evangelium, vade, praedica populo tibi commisso."

11. Hefele-LeClercq, II, 565; Hardouin, *Acta Conciliorum et Epistolae Decretales ac Constitutiones Summorum Pontificum* (12 vols., Parisiis, 1714-1715), III, 1670 (hereafter cited Hardouin).

12. Hardouin, III, 1670.

13. *Monumenta Germaniae Historica,* Legum Sectio II, *Capitularia Regum Francorum,* I (ed. A. Boretius, Hannoverae, 1883), 45; 61.

the bishops were earnestly urged to fulfill their obligation in regard to preaching.[14] Even though particular synods in the tenth century, such as that of Hohenaltheim (916),[15] urged bishops to look faithfully to the fulfillment of their obligation of preaching, nevertheless the actual conditions of the time did not prove favorable for full obedience to these laws. There were, nevertheless, instances of apostolic preaching activity, as in the case of St. Wolfgang, Bishop of Regensburg (972-994). But inasmuch as the Church in the eleventh century primarily devoted itself to the inner development of its religious worship, little mention is found, whether in general or in particular legislation, of the preaching office in the Church, and accordingly the legislation regarding the work of preaching must have been meager, if not almost entirely wanting.[16]

b. Priests

Although the preaching office was considered as inherent in the episcopate, yet in the East the task of preaching was assumed by priests at an early period in the Church's history, as the Apostolic Constitutions demonstrate.[17] Since Catholicism in the East spread in the rural sections as well as in the large cities, the bishops of necessity appointed priests to perform the work of preaching in the rural areas. Palladius (ca. 365-431) in his biography of St. John Chrysostom (354-407) remarked that St. John while yet a priest preached in place of his bishop, even in the episcopal city.

It was only a short time later that priests began to preach in the West. No doubt the practice was derived from the East. The Church of the East wielded a particular influence on the African Church.[18] St. Augustine (354-430), while a priest, fulfilled the obligation of preaching for his bishop, Valerius (+396). The latter, being a Greek and not

14. *MGH,* Legum Sectio II, *Capitularia Regum Francorum,* I, 153.

15. *MGH,* Legum ectio II, *Capitularia Regum Francorum,* I, 153; Mansi, *Sacrorum Conciliorum Nova et Amplissima Collectio* (53 vols. in 60, Parisiis, 1901-1927), XVII, 326 (hereafter cited Mansi).

16. *MGH, Scriptores,* IV (ed. G. Pertz, 1841), 546-548; Hinschius, *Das Kirchenrecht der Katholiken und Protestanten in Deutschland* (6 vols., Berlin, 1869-1897), IV, 449 (hereafter cited *Das Kirchenrecht*).

17. *Constitutiones Apostolicae,* Lib. II, cap. 57, 9; Funk, *Didascalia et Constitutiones Apostolorum* (2 vols., Paderbornae, 1905), I, 162-163.

18. Thomassinus, *Vetus et Nova Ecclesiae Disciplina circa Beneficia et Beneficiarios* (10 vols., Magontiaci, 1787), VI, Pars II, lib. III, cap. LXXXIII, nn. 4, 8 (hereafter cited Thomassinus).

conversant in the Latin language, had found it difficult to preach to his people.[19]

When the heresies began to arise, and especially after the Arian heresy, the priests in Africa as well as in the East were forbidden to preach. St. Jerome (342-420) vehemently assailed the bishops of Africa for refusing to allow the priests to preach in their presence.[20] This refusal, however, was simply invoked as a protective measure at the time. It was not a standing practice among the bishops to deny preaching faculties to their priests.

In the sixth century there was enacted definite legislation which determined that priests should preach. In the II Council of Vaison (529)[21] the practice which called upon priests to preach was confirmed and extended even to rural parishes. Caesarius (470-542), Bishop of Arles (502-542), held that it was a sacred and inexorable law that in virtue of their office bishops had to discharge the obligation of preaching either through themselves or through their priests.[22]

The Capitularies of Charlemagne in the eighth and early ninth centuries, in reminding the bishops of their obligation to preach, admonished them to send to the parishes capable priests who would preach and instruct the people in those things which were necessary for salvation.[23] About the year 762 Chrodegang (ca. 705-766), Bishop of Metz (742-766), in his *Regula Canonicorum*[24] enjoined preaching in all the churches of his diocese, twice a month at the least; or better still, on every feast day and Sunday. He likewise ordered that the preaching should be adapted to the people's understanding.[25] Theodulph (761-821), Bishop of Orleans (798-818), in two capitularies urged his priests to preach especially on Sunday; even those who were not able to interpret

19. Schleiniger, *Das kirchliche Predigtamt* (3. ed., Freiburg im Breisgau: Herder, 1881), p. 15.

20. *Epistola LII* (Ad Neoptianum) — Migne, *Patrologiae Cursus Completus, Series Latina* (221 vols., Parisiis, 1844-1864), XXII, 534 (hereafter cited *MPL*); Cf. Schleiniger, *Das kirchliche Predigtamt*, p. 15.

21. Mansi, VIII, 727.

22. Thomassinus, VI, Pars II, lib. I, cap. LXXXIX, n. 9.

23. *MGH*, Legum Sectio II, *Capitularia Regum Francorum*, I, 45, 61.

24. Mansi, XIV, 337.

25. Dargan, *A History of Preaching* (New York: A. C. Armstrong and Co., 1905), p. 134.

the Scriptures according to the Fathers were nevertheless to preach the things that were necessary for salvation.[26]

In the ninth century, in the first Capitulary of the *Missi* of Aachen,[27] the priests were earnestly urged to fulfill their obligation of preaching. The same regulations were expressed in the Councils of Mainz (813), Meux (845) and Valence (855).[28]

c. Deacons

According to Holy Scripture deacons exercised the office of preaching.[29] This practice however did not last long. As the Church extended in its development the deacons became dependent upon the bishops for preaching. Already in the third century they were partly forbidden to preach.[30] Nevertheless the deacons could preach with the permission of the bishop. Since the seventh century the law which made it allowable for deacons to preach has remained the same down to the present time.[31]

d. Laymen

It is evident both from Scripture and Church history that laymen did preach in the first three centuries of the Church. They were those who were especially endowed with the *charismata.* As an example of a particular layman who preached, one may point to Origen (185-254).[32] Canon 98 of the *Statuta Ecclesiae Antiqua*[33] presupposed that laymen could preach.

Even though Pope St. Leo I (440-461) in a letter to Theodoret (ca. 393- ca . 458), Bishop of Cyrrhus in Syria (ca. 423 - ca. 458), had, because of the conditions of the Church at that time, forbidden laymen

26. *Realencyklopaedie fuer protestantische Theologie und Kirche* (3. ed., ed. A. Hauck, 24 vols., Leipzig, 1896-1913), s. v. *Theodulph.*

27. *MGH,* Legum Sectio II, *Capitularia Regum Francorum,* I, 153.

28. Mansi, XIV, 72 (c. 25); 826 (c. 35); Hefele-LeClercq, IV, 208.

29. Acts, VI:1-6; VII:1-56; VIII:5-40.

30. Hinschius, *Das Kirchenrecht,* IV, 451.

31. Hinschius, *loc. cit.*

32. Hinschius, *ibid.,* p. 450.

33. "Laicus praesentibus clericis nisi ipsis jubentibus docere non audeat." — Bruns, *Canones Apostolorum et Conciliorum Saeculorum IV-VII* (2 vols., Berolini: G. Reimeri, 1839), I, 150.

to preach, this legislation was not definite.[34] Laymen definitely were excluded from the office of preaching only some centuries later in the IV General Council of the Lateran (1215).[35]

ARTICLE 3. *The Subject Matter of Preaching*

In the early days of the Church, when the faithful met for worship the Scriptures were read by the bishop, who thereupon added admonitions in which he encouraged them to live according to the teachings of the gospel. Later the Fathers developed the homily.[36]

The word homily comes from the Greek and signified a discourse or converse. It came to mean a religious discourse which expounded in an analytical method a paragraph or verse of Scripture.

A sermon, on the other hand, was a synthetic discourse which developed a definite theme.[37] The first synthetic discourse or sermon appeared in connection with the celebration of the feasts of martyrs. From the fourth century onward, such sermons consisted of a single idea rhetorically developed in explanation of some truth of the faith against the heretics. Sermons were likewise given on particular occasions, such as the consecration of a bishop and the conducting of funerals. Still later, sermons became associated with the Mass. This latter practice has continued into the present.[38] Throughout the centuries particular legislation often determined the nature of the sermon for the occasions on which it was preached.

Charlemagne urged the preachers of his time not only to use the homilies of the Fathers, but particularly to teach the dogmas of the faith as contained in the Apostles' Creed. In his Capitulary of 789 he listed the truths which were to constitute the subject of preaching.[39]

---

34. Jaffe, *Regesta Pontificum Romanorum ab condita Ecclesia ad annum post Christum natum MCXCVIII* (2. ed. correctam et auctam auspiciis Gulielmi Wattenbach, curaverunt F. Kaltenbrunner, P. Ewald, S. Loewenfeld, 2 vols. in 1, Lipsiae, 1885-1888), n. 496 (hereafter cited as JK for documents up to 590, as JE for documents from 590 to 882, and as JL for documents from 882 to 1198).

35. IV General Council of the Lateran (1215), c. 3—c. 13, § 6, X, *de haereticis*, V, 7. Hinschius (*Das Kirchenrecht*, IV, 451) declared that this legislation in practice definitely excluded laymen from preaching.

36. Hinschius, *Das Kirchenrecht*, IV, 449.

37. *A New English Dictionary on Historical Principles*, s. v. *homily*.

38. Hinschius, *Das Kirchenrecht*, IV, 449.

39. *MGH*, Legum Sectio II, *Capitularia Regum Francorum*, I, 45.

The Council of Tours in 813 ordered that each preacher should strive to translate the homilies into the vernacular, in order that all the people might the more readily understand what was addressed to them.[40]

40. Dargan, *A History of Preaching*, pp. 165-167.

Chapter II

GRATIAN AND THE DECRETAL LAW

The legislation in regard to preaching during the five centuries preceding the Council of Trent (1545-1563) was a continuation of the law of the antecedent era. This legislation may be considered under three separate articles: 1) the continuation of the legislative measures by means of which priests, as the shepherds of souls, were through their preaching to prevent abuses and to elaborate the doctrinal instructions given in the parish churches; 2) the laws enacted against the irregular preaching undertaken by heretics and their sympathizers; and 3) the privileges of the new Orders of preaching friars, and the legislation which sought to keep their activities within the framework of the Church's organization. To each of these articles there will be given some closer and more specific consideration.

Article 1. *Continuation of Legislation for Pastors to Preach*

In the *Decree* of Gratian (+ca. 1160) mention was made of the letter written by Pope St. Leo I (440-461) to Theodoret (ca. 393 - ca. 458), Bishop of Cyrrhus in Syria (ca. 423 - ca. 458), in which letter the Supreme Pontiff ordered that no one should preach, whether a monk or layman, unless he was a priest.[1] However, the glossator[2] stated that this decree of Pope St. Leo I was not contrary to the fact that deacons could preach[3] when their act of preaching was the equivalent of an act of reading in public to the faithful. Nor was it contrary to the fact that laymen could preach if they had obtained the permission of the ecclesiastical superior.[4]

The question also arose whether a subdeacon or others in Minor Orders could preach. According to the Decretals of Pope Gregory IX (1227-1241) it was possible for a subdeacon and those in Minor Orders to preach.[5] Since subdeacons and those who were in Minor Orders could

1. JK, n. 496,
2. *Glossa ordinaria, causus* ad c. 19, C. XVI, q. 1, s. v. *Adiicimus.*
3. C. 2, D. XCII; Cf. Migne, *MPL,* LXXVII, 1335.
4. Cans. 98 and 99 of the IV Council of Carthage (398)—Bruns, I, 150; c. 29, D. XXIII.
5. C. 5, X, *de aetate et qualitate et ordine praeficiendorum,* I, 14; JL, n. 14219.

by way of dispensation have part in the care of souls, they could in consequence be given also a share in the work of preaching. However, they then preached not by reason of the Order received, but by reason of the jurisdiction granted to them. Moreover, in such cases those who had part in the care of souls were to receive ordination to the priesthood or else lose the advanced standing they had.[6]

According to a canon enacted in the III General Council of the Lateran (1179), the bishop was commanded to confer the care of souls only upon those who had attained twenty-five years of age, and met also the requirements of the sacred canons regarding the matter of due knowledge and commendable morals. The ones appointed were obliged to receive the corresponding Order within six months or be removed from office.[7]

For such cities and dioceses in which there were people of diverse languages the IV General Council of the Lateran (1215) in its ninth canon decreed that bishops should provide suitable men who, according to the different rites and languages, would be able to administer the sacraments and to instruct the people by word and example.[8] The bishop was to provide these men at his own expense.[9] If necessity required it, the bishop was furthermore to appoint a special vicar general. Hostiensis (1271) declared that such a vicar general possessed ordinary jurisdiction, but that his status remained subordinate to that of the bishop of the diocese.[10] The conciliar decree branded with excommunication anyone who on his own authority and without acknowledging subjection to the bishop appropriated the office of vicar to himself.[11]

The Fathers of the IV General Council of the Lateran were keenly conscious of the great necessity of sermon preaching. In giving expression to this consciousness they availed themselves of a strong comparison. Just as material food was indispensable for the human body, so spiritual food

---

6. C. 1, X, *de aetate et qualitate et ordine praeficiendorum*, I, 14.

7. III General Council of the Lateran, c. 3—Schroeder, *Disciplinary Decrees of the General Councils* (St. Louis, Mo.: Herder, 1937), pp. 216-217 (hereafter cited *Disciplinary Decrees*).

8. C. 14, X, *de officio iudicis ordinarii*, I, 31.

9. *Glossa ordinaria*, ad c. 14, X, *de officio iudicis ordinarii*, I, 31 s.v. *provideant*.

10. Hostiensis (Henricus de Segusia), *Commentaria in Quinque Decretalium Libros* (5 vols. in 3, Venetiis, 1581), Lib. I, tit. *De officio archidiaconi*, cap. I, s. v. *Vicarium*, n. 1.

11. C. 14, X, *de officio indicis ordinarii*, I, 31; Cf. Schroeder, *Disciplinary Decrees*, pp. 250-251.

was imperative for the proper nourishment of the soul, since "not by bread alone doth man live, but in every word that proceedeth from the mouth of God."[12]

Accordingly, the Council decreed that in the event that bishops found it impossible, in view of their multiplied obligations, as a result of their bodily infirmities, or in consequence of some hostile invasion, to break the bread of doctrine through their personal ministry of preaching, then they were to provide in their stead capable and qualified men, powerful in word and example, who could fruitfully exercise the office of preaching. The Council in addition required the bishops to ensure a due compensation for the ones whom they authorized with the office of preaching, in order that no occasion be offered for any desistence from their task.

Also according to this canon 10 of the Council, bishops were to appoint, in cathedral and conventual churches alike, men who were suited to function as their assistants in the important office of preaching.[13] The office of preaching thus was recognized as a privileged one.[14] Consequently, in order to exercise the office of preaching, monks were in need of the bishop's previous approbation.[15]

Particular legislation during the twelfth and thirteenth centuries sought to inculcate the general regulations of the Church. A council which was held in Gran, Hungary, in the year 1114 commanded in its second canon that the epistle and gospel be explained to the people every Sunday in the larger churches, and that the *Creed* and the *Lord's Prayer* be explained in the smaller churches.[16]

The Council of Oxford (1222) urged the priests of all parish churches strictly to fulfill their obligation of preaching the word of God to the people committed to their care.[17]

---

12. Matth., IV:4.

13. C. 15, X, *de officio iudicis ordinarii,* I, 31; Cf. Schroeder, *Disciplinary Decrees,* pp. 251-252.

14. *Glossa ordinaria,* ad c. 15, X, *de officio iudicis ordinarii,* I, 31, s. v. *praedicationis officium.*

15. C. 5, X, *de statu monachorum et canonicorum regularium,* III, 35; Potthast, *Regesta Pontificum Romanorum inde ab anno post Christum natum MCXCVIII ad annum MCCCIV* (2 vols., Berolini, 1874-1875), n. 1329 (hereafter cited Potthast); c. 13, § 6, X, *de haereticis,* V, 7.

16. Hefele-LeClercq, V, 542; Mansi, XXI, 99 (c. 2).

17. Mansi, XXII, 1154 (c. 9).

The Provincial Council of Trier (1227) commanded priests to teach their people what constituted a mortal sin and, in general, to instruct them in the articles of faith and in the ten commandments.[18]

Likewise, the Provincial Council of Beziers (1246) and the Council of Albi (1254) ordered all parish priests, either personally or through others, to explain the articles of faith to the people in a simple and intelligible manner every Sunday and feast day, so that no one could excusably be ignorant of these salutary truths.[19]

In England the Council of Lambeth (1282) ordered that every priest in a parish should explain to the people in the vernacular the articles of faith, the ten commandments, the precepts of the gospel, the seven works of mercy, the seven capital sins, the seven principal virtues, and the seven sacraments. This Council declared that the priests could not plead ignorance regarding these truths, since brief summaries of these Catholic tenets had been issued to them.[20]

Such a summary of Christian doctrine was published by a provincial council which was held at Lavaur in 1368. The priests were commanded to use this summary in their explanation of the truths of the Catholic faith to the people every Sunday and feast day.[21]

In the following century the Council of Tortosa in Spain (1429) similarly commanded that such a compendium of christian doctrine be made, and that it then be used in the explanation to the people every Sunday of the truths of the faith.[22] The decrees of the Council of Toledo (1473) were similar to those of Tortosa.[23]

ARTICLE 2.

Irregularities in Preaching: The Heretics and their Sympathizers

Irregularities crept into the exercise of the preaching office in two different ways: first, through a behavior in the pulpit which was incon-

---

18. Mansi, XXIII, 31 (c. 8).

19. Mansi, XXIII, 693 (c. 7); XXIII, 836-837 (c. 17 and c. 18); Cf. *Dictionnaire de Theologie Catholique* (ed. E. Vacant [+1901], E. Mangenot [+1922] and E. Amann [1880-1948], 28 vols. incomplete, Paris: Letouzey et Ane, 1903-1946), II, 1899.

20. Mansi, XXIV, 410-413 (c. 10).

21. Mansi, XXVI, 484-493 (c. 1); Cf. *Dictionnaire de Theologie Catholique,* II, 1902.

22. Mansi, XXVIII, 1147-1148 (c. 6).

23. Mansi, XXXII, 392 (c. 13).

sistent with the proper decorum and dignity in preaching and secondly, through a usurpation of the office of preaching in that the necessary authorization from the proper ecclesiastical superiors was not obtained. Misconduct in the preaching of sermons was profoundly condemned and censured by the Church, as is evident from the decrees promulgated in some of the particular councils.

The Council of Tours (1448), which was held at Angers, declared that preachers, regardless of their state or condition, were not to preach in buildings specifically erected as theaters; they could preach solely in the House of God, with the reverence and the humility befitted the sacred occasion.[24] The Council further declared in its decrees that those who had obtained permission or authorization for preaching were not, despite whatever status, rank or order they enjoyed, to employ specially constructed stages when they preached either in public or in other accustomed places. With due consideration for the demands inherent in the requisite reverence and humility, those who preached were not to make use of loud cries, of savage shouting, of impetuous conduct, or of extravagant gestures in the sacred temple of God.[25]

The Archbishop of Sens, in a council held in 1528, instructed his suffragans to restrain preachers from using in their sermons passages taken from the profane law, useless excerpts drawn from poetry, and references dealing with subtle or inane questions. Furthermore, if preachers excited the people to loud laughter through the recitation of ridiculous and gossipy stories in the manner of a jester, or tried to dissuade the people from obeying their proper ecclesiastical superiors, they were to be suspended from the office of preaching.[26] In his historical study relative to preaching, Dargan stated that such buffoonery in preaching was practiced in many places during the late fifteenth and early sixteenth centuries.[27]

To counteract the practice of such indecorous behavior in pulpit oratory, the Church in particular places began to enact laws which more specifically determined the needed qualifications of the preacher. In Italy the Council of Ravenna (1311) legislated that the preacher should be a

24. Mansi, XXXII, 75 (c. 6).
25. Mansi, XXXII, 81, (c. 6).
26. Mansi, XXXII, 1198-1199, *Index decretorum ad mores pertinentium*, c. 35.
27. Dargan, *A History of Preaching*, pp. 307-308.

person at least thirty years of age, and that he should be one who was respected for his good morals, his holiness, and his knowledge.[28]

In Germany the same kind of legislation was enacted in the Provincial Council of Cologne (1536).[29]

In France similar decrees emanated from the Provincial Council of Narbonne (1551).[30]

An important document concerning the necessary qualifications for a preacher was the constitution issued by Pope Leo X (1513-1521) in the V General Council of the Lateran (1512-1517),[31] in which he decreed and ordained

> that no clerics, whether seculars or members of any of the mendicant orders or any other order to which the office of preaching pertains by right, custom, privilege, or otherwise, be admitted to exercise that office unless they have first been carefully examined by their respective superiors and found competent and fit as regards moral integrity, age, knowledge, uprightness, prudence, and exemplariness of life. Of this approved competency they must, wherever they may preach, acquaint the local ordinary by means of authentic letters or other instruments from those who examined and approved them for this work.[32]

The age was one in which lay persons as well as heretics usurped the office of preaching. In its legislation the Church sought earnestly to prevent discord within its ranks. In the city of Metz certain lay persons heretically expounded Holy Scripture and assumed the office of preaching. Likewise they held secret conventions in which they mocked the simplicity of the priests and spurned those who did not belong to their own group. Pope Innocent III (1198-1216) reproved them for holding such secret conferences, indicating to them that Christ hated the works of darkness, for when He sent His Apostles forth to preach, He com-

---

28. Mansi, XXV, 457 (c. 13).
29. Mansi, XXXII, 1246 (Pars V, cc. 1 and 2); 1249-1255 (Pars VI, cc. 8-13).
30. Mansi, XXXIII, 1264 (c. 35).
31. Leo X (in Conc. Lateranen. V), const. *Supernae maiestatis*, § 1, 19 dec. 1516—*Codicis Iuris Canonici Fontes*, cura Emi Petri Card. Gasparri editi (9 vols., Romae [postea Civitate Vaticana]: Typis Polyglottis Vaticanis, 1923-1939) (Vols. VII-IX, ed. cura et studio Emi Iustiniani Card. Seredi), n. 71 (hereafter cited *Fontes*).
32. Schroeder, *Disciplinary Decrees*, p. 505.

manded them: "What you hear whispered, preach it on the housetops."[33] Moreover, the Pope most forcefully condemned their usurpation of the preaching office.[34] Pope Innocent therefore forbade laymen to preach or to hold secret conventions.[35]

The same Pope in another letter to certain bishops assailed the practice of an abbess who in their dioceses had assumed the right of blessing her nuns, of hearing their confessions, and of preaching to them. The Pope urged the bishops to see that such malfeasance and usurpation of office cease immediately, since it so absurdly proved contrary to the teaching of the Church. Even though the Blessed Virgin Mary was more worthy and exalted than the Apostles, so wrote the Pope, nevertheless it was not to her but to the Apostles that Christ gave the power of the keys.[36]

Pope Gregory IX (1227-1241) in a letter to the Archbishop of Milan likewise commanded that laymen desist from usurping the office of preaching.[37] Already in the IV General Council of the Lateran (1215) it had been declared that those who without any authorization from the Holy See or from the Catholic bishop of the locality assumed the preaching office, and presumed to preach publicly or privately, thereby incurred excommunication.[38]

The seekers of alms, some of whom were prone to misrepresent themselves and to preach certain abuses, were forbidden to be admitted anywhere for preaching unless they exhibited genuine documents of such authorization either from the Apostolic See or from the bishop of the locality, in which case they could preach solely in accordance with the content of the letters.[39]

Particular councils which were held throughout the different parts of the world contemporaneously with the IV General Council of the Lateran also forbade the admission of alms-seekers to the office of preaching unless they exhibited such letters from the proper ecclesiastical authority.

---

33. Matth., X:27.
34. *Glossa ordinaria, casus* ad c. 12, X, *de haereticis,* V, 7, s.v. *Quidam laici.*
35. Potthast, n. 780.
36. C. 10, X, *de poenitentiis et remissionibus,* V, 38.
37. Potthast, n. 9675; c. 14, X, *de haereticis,* V, 7.
38. Canon 3—Schroeder, *Disciplinary Decrees,* p. 244.
39. C. 14, X, *de poenitentiis et remissionibus,* V, 38; IV General Council of the Lateran (1215), c. 62—Schroeder, *Disciplinary Decrees,* p. 287.

Such was the decree of the Council of Paris (1212).[40] Richard Poore (+1237), Bishop of Salisbury, England (1217-1228), also issued such a decree in his constitutions of 1217.[41] Similar legislation was adopted in the Council of Beziers (1246).[42] and that of Buda (1279) in Hungary.[43]

Further enactments of the Church concerning preaching were made specifically against certain heretics. Pope Innocent III (1298-1216) proclaimed the necessity of preaching, and the fact that one must have the authorization of the supreme pontiff or of some other prelate to exercise this office, against the heresy of the Waldensians.[44] The IV General Council of the Lateran (1215) condemned the errors in the preaching of Joachim (ca. 1132-1202), Abbot of Flora in Calabria.[45] Likewise Pope Martin V (1417-1431) in the General Council of Constance (1414-1418) condemned certain errors of Wicliffe (1324-1384) and Huss (ca. 1369-1415) relative to the matter of preaching.[46]

ARTICLE 3. *Privileges of the Preaching Friars*

In the early part of the thirteenth century there arose in the Church two Religious Orders, namely the Franciscans and Dominicans, whose purpose was particularly that of preaching. Pope Innocent III (1198-1216) gave permission to St. Francis of Assisi (1182-1226) and his brothers to preach penance and moral sermons.[47] The very purpose for founding the Dominicans was to preach against the Albigensian heresy.[48] It is no wonder, then, that Pope Gregory IX (1227-1241) already in 1227 granted to the Dominicans the privilege of preaching everywhere, even in parish churches.[49]

---

40. Mansi, XXII, 821 (c. 8).
41. Mansi, XXII, 1123 (c. 50).
42. Mansi, XXIII, 692-693 (c. 5).
43. Mansi, XXIV, 283-284 (c. 27).
44 Innocentius III, ep. *Eius exemplo,* 18 dec. 1208, Professio fidei Waldensibus praescripta — *Fontes,* n. 30.
45. IV General Council of the Lateran (1215), c. 2; c. 13, X, *de haereticis,* V, 7; Hefele-LeClercq, V, 1328.
46. Martinus V (in Conc. Constantien.), const. *Inter cunctas,* 22 febr. 1418, art. 14, Joannis Wicleff, damn., art. 17, 18, Joannis Huss, damn., art. 38, *Interrogatorium iuxta quod de haeresi suspecti interrogari debent.* — *Fontes,* n. 43.
47. Heimbucher, *Die Orden und Kongregationen der katholischen Kirche* (3. ed., 2 vols., Paderborn: Verlag Ferdinand Schoeningh, 1933-1934), I, 672.
48. Heimbucher, *op. cit.*. I, 479.
49. Potthast, nn. 8042, 8043.

That this granted permission really implied a privilege is evident from the fact that in the beginning these Friars were laymen, and hence bound by the earlier legislation, namely that laymen should not preach.[50] The same kind of privilege was extended to the Franciscans by Pope Gregory IX in 1237.[51]

The preaching Friars, however, abused the privileges granted to them. As a result there arose an enmity between the newly-founded Religious Orders and the secular clergy. Many complaints from the secular clergy were made to Pope Innocent IV (1243-1254). The Pope however ignored the complaints, and renewed the privileges granted by Pope Gregory IX. Moreover, Pope Innocent IV brought charges of oppression of the Religious Orders against the prelates and others, and insisted the discontinuance of such oppression.[52] However, two weeks before his death Pope Innocent IV issued a decree which ordered that the Friars were not to preach in their monastery churches before or during the parish church Mass. Moreover, they were not to preach in the parish church unless they had the permission of the pastor; and they likewise were to forego preaching on the same day in a place where the local ordinary or his representative preached.[53]

Pope Alexander IV (1254-1261), a few months later, again gave back many privileges to the Orders. He allowed them to preach everywhere merely with the permission of the bishop or of the papal legate.[54]

These privileges were extended even more by Pope Martin IV (1281-1285) in 1282, when he ruled that even the permission of the local ordinary or of the papal legate was no longer needed. The members of the Religious Orders could preach everywhere. The only necessary qualification according to his legislation was that each member had undergone an examination and had then received the approval of his minister general, or of the provincial with the consent of his council members.[55]

Thus the struggle between the Religious Orders and the secular clergy remained, and in bitterness it grew even greater. This is evident

50. C. 19, C. XVI, q. 1.
51. Potthast, nn. 10316, 10386.
52. Cc. 16, 17, X, *de excessibus praelatorum et subditorum*, V, 31.
53. Potthast, n. 15562.
54. Potthast, nn. 15602. 17452.
55. Potthast, nn. 21837, 21836.

from the decrees of local synods and councils. For instance, The Council of Milan (1287) declared that whenever it was doubtful whether the Order had such a privilege, the bishop should demand proof.[56] Furthermore, the Council of Mainz (1261) forbade the Friars to preach to the people at the time when processions were being held in the parish churches.[57]

To put an end to this altercation and discord between the Orders and the secular clergy, Pope Boniface VIII (1294-1303) limited the privileges of the preaching Friars somewhat in his decretal *Super cathedram.*[58] This decretal ordered that the Dominicans and Franciscans could preach in their own churches and in public except at that hour during which the local ordinary or his representative solemnly preached. Moreover, they could preach at funerals and on the special feast days of their Order unless the bishop had ordered the members of the clergy to meet at that time. In the parish churches the Friars were not to preach unless they had been invited to do so by the pastor, and thus had the pastor's permission, or unless the bishop had commanded the Friars to preach.

This legislation was not long in force, for Pope Benedict XI (1303-1304) in his decretal *Inter cunctas*[59] abrogated the constitution of Boniface VIII. In his decretal Benedict XI returned the former privileges to the Orders. But even by the law of this decretal the Friars could not preach in parish churches unless they had obtained the permission of the pastor.

Pope Clement V (1305-1314) in the Council of Vienne (1311-1312) restored the decretal of Boniface VIII in regard to preaching.[60] There are exstant two decrees of Clement V, which some consider as not really conciliar legislation that proceeded from the Council of Vienne, for it seems that they were not enacted in the Council.[61] The one decree enumerated thirty complaints of the Religious Ordrs against episcopal

---

56. Mansi, XXIV, 880 (c. 27).
57. Mansi, XXIII, 1100 (c. 45).
58. C. 2, *de sepulturis,* III, 7, in Clem.; Potthast, n. 24913; cf. Schroeder, *Disciplinary Decrees,* p. 379.
59. C. 1, *de privilegiis,* V, 7, in Extravag. com.; Potthast, n. 25370.
60. C. 2, *de supulturis,* V, 7, in Clem.; Potthast, n. 24913; cf. Schroeder, *Disciplinary Decrees,* p. 379.
61. Schroeder, *Disciplinary Decrees,* pp. 433-434; cf. Mueller, *Das Konzil von Vienne 1311-1312, Seine Quellen und seine Geschichte* (Muenster in Westfalen: Aschendorff Verlag, 1934), p. 687.

oppression.[62] The other decree recounted seven complaints of the bishops and prelates against the Religious Orders.[63] These show the strife that yet existed between the religious and the secular clergy. Again, there were instances in which particular legislation sought to modify the privileges possessed by the religious. Such attempts were in evidence in the Council of Mainz (1310)[64] and in the Council of Ravenna (1311).[65] However, the Pope protected the rightful claims of the Religious Orders, and asked the bishops to recognize the privileges that had been granted to them.[66]

In general the law enacted in the Council of Vienne remained the same until the V General Council of the Lateran (1512-1517). This latter Council ordered that every Friar or religious be first examined by his superior, and only then be presented to the local ordinary with due evidence of the approved competency for preaching.[67]

62. C. un., *de excessibus praelatorum*, V, 6, in Clem.
63. C. 1, *de privilegiis et excessibus privilegiatorum*, V. 7, in Clem.
64. Mansi, XXV, 345, *De privilegiis privilegiatorum.*
65. Mansi, XXV, 457 (c. 13).
66. Potthast, nn. 25387, 25388.
67. Leo X (in Conc. Lateranen. V), const. *Supernae maiestatis*, 19 dec. 1516, § 1 — *Fontes*, n. 71; cf. Schroeder, *Disciplinary Decrees*, p. 505.

CHAPTER III

FROM THE COUNCIL OF TRENT (1545-1563) TO THE CODE OF CANON LAW (1918)

ARTICLE 1. *The Obligation of Preaching on the Part of Pastors*

a. The Obligation of Preaching

The Council of Trent, realizing the importance of preaching and its necessity for the Christian commonweal, decreed that archpriests, priests and all others who had charge of parochial churches and of other churches to which was attached the care of souls had also the obligation of preaching at least on the Sundays and feast days.[1] The Council further declared that this obligation was primarily a personal one.[2]

As early as 1591 the Sacred Congregation of the Council explained that it was not with reference to other churches, but with reference to their own parish churches, that pastors were obliged to exercise the office of preaching. Moreover, when preaching in their own parishes the pastors could not demand a stipend, since the duty of preaching there was part of their office.[3] The same Congregation some years later declared that the pastors could not demand a stipend for preaching in their own parish churches even for reason of poverty.[4]

Barbosa (1589-1649) proclaimed that the exercise of preaching was a personal obligation of the pastor,[5] as also did Schmalzgrueber (1663-1735).[6]

The pastor's obligation of preaching, however, was not so strictly personal that he could not supplant his work through that of a substitute. In fact, the Council of Trent decreed that other competent priests should

1. Conc. Trident., sess. V, *de ref.*, c. 2; cf. Schroeder, *Canons and Decrees of the Council of Trent* (St. Louis, Mo.: B. Herder Book Co., 1941), pp. 305-306 (hereafter cited *Council of Trent.*).

2. Conc. Trident., sess. V, *de ref.*, c. 2; sess. XXIV, *de ref.*, c. 4.

3. S.C.C., *Barcinonen.*, 22 mart. 1591, ad 1 — *Fontes*, n. 2224.

4. S.C.C., *Vestana*, 10 mart. 1621 — Ferraris, *Prompta Bibliotheca Canonica, Iuridica, Moralis, Theologica, necnon Ascetica, Polemica, Rubricistica, Historica* (ed. noviss., 9 vols., Romae, 1885-1899), s. v. *Parochus*, art. II, n. 77 (hereafter cited *Bibliotheca).*

5. *Pastoralis Solicitudinis sive Tripartita Descriptio de Officio et Potestate Parochi* (5. ed., Lugduni, 1665), Pars I, cap. XIV, n. 5 (hereafter cited *De Officio et Potestate Parochi).*

6. *Ius Ecclesiasticum Universum* (5 vols. in 12, Romae, 1843-1845), Lib. III, tit. 29, n. 12.

be appointed when the pastor was hindered from fulfilling his duty.[7] The Council did not determine the causes for which one might consider himself impeded or hindered.

Pignatelli (ca. 1695) declared that, when there was occasion for the pastor to utilize the services of a substitute, the pastor was obliged to pay for the services rendered.[8] The substitute whom the pastor selected in his stead needed the pemission and approbation of the local ordinary.[9] However, the pastor could allow a priest who was known to him, whether secular or regular, to preach once or twice in his church without the approbation of the local ordinary.[10]

Throughout the centuries following the Council of Trent, the Popes often stressed the necessity of adhering to the law of the Council in regard to preaching.

Pope Innocent XIII (1721-1724) in writing to the hierarchy of Spain complained about the conduct of those priests who had the care of souls and yet failed to preach. He strictly commanded every Archbishop and Bishop of Spain to see to it that all who had the care of souls, unless they were legitimately hindered, fulfilled their obligation of preaching personally, or through other capable men. If the pastors or those who had the care of souls were not capable of fulfilling this duty, then the bishops were to appoint others to take their place in preaching; and these substitutes were to receive a proper compensation from the pastors. Moreover, in the future parochial benefices were to be conferred on only such priests as were able and fit to perform the duty of preaching.[11]

Pope Benedict XIII (1724-1730) in two constitutions called to mind the obligation of preaching on the part of pastors and of those priests to whom was entrusted the care of souls by urging in particular the fulfillment of the law of his predecessor.[12]

Pope Benedict XIV (1740-1758) in his Encylical Letter *Ubi primum* of 1740 ordered that only worthy and capable priests be placed in

7. Conc. Trident., sess. V, *de ref.*, c. 2; sess. XXIV, *de ref.*, c. 4.

8. S.C. Ep. et Reg., *Faventina*, 17 mart. 1602 — Pignatelli, *Consultationes Canonicae* (10 vols. in 5, Coloniae Allobrogorum, 1700), IV, cons. 206, n. 58.

9. Barbosa, *De Officio et Potestate Parochi*, Pars I, cap. XIV, n. 8.

10. Barbosa, *loc. cit.*

11. Innocentius XIII, const. *Apostolici ministerii*, 23 maii 1723, § 11 — *Fontes*, n. 280.

12. Benedictus XIII, const. *In supremo*, 23 sept. 1724, § § 8, 28, — *Fontes*, n. 283; Benedictus XIII, const. *Pastoralis officii*, 27 mart. 1726, § 3 — *Fontes*, n. 292.

parishes, and that on Sundays and feast days of precept they not only preach within the understanding of the people all the things necessary for salvation, but also instruct the children in the catechism.[13] Benedict XIV further decreed that in their episcopal and canonical visitations the bishops were diligently to inquire whether the pastors had fulfilled the requirements of the Council of Trent in regard to preaching.[14]

A century later, Pope Pius IX (1846-1878) in an encyclical letter of 1846 urged the bishops and priests to be faithful to their obligation of preaching to their flock, so that the people might the better be able to work out their salvation.[15]

Pope Pius X (1903-1914) in an encyclical letter issued in 1905 again stressed the fact that the Council of Trent had obliged priests who had the care of souls to preach on Sundays and feast days.[16]

Pope Benedict XV (1914-1922) called attention to the obligation of preaching in his Encylical Letter *Humani generis* of 1917. He particularly reminded the bishops of their duty to exclude unworthy preachers and to choose, train and direct worthy ones, so that there might be, not more preachers, but more preachers according to God. He placed St. Paul before their eyes as the example of a perfect preacher.[17]

b. The Time

The Council of Trent not only had placed an obligation of preaching on those who had the care of souls, but the Council also had determined the time at which this obligation was binding. It decreed that pastors should preach in their parish churches on at least every Sunday and on the solemn feast days.[18]

Again, the Council of Trent declared that parish priests were to announce the Sacred Scriptures and the divine law at least on Sundays and on the solemn feast days. This was to be done daily or at least three times a week during the penitential seasons of Lent and Advent, or as often as the bishop judged it necessary. If the parish priests were hindered from fulfilling this obligation, then others were to be appointed by the bishop

13. Benedictus XIV, ep. encycl. *Ubi primum*, 3 dec. 1740, § 3 — *Fontes*, n. 304.
14. Benedictus XIV, const. *Firmandis*, 6 nov. 1744, § 9 — *Fontes*, n. 349.
15. Pius IX, ep. encyvl. *Qui pluribus*, 8 nov. 1846, § 7 — *Fontes*, n. 504.
16. Pius X, litt. encycl. *Acerbo nimis*, 15 apr. 1905, n. 11 — *Fontes*, n. 666.
17. Benedictus XV, litt. encycl. *Humani generis*, 15 iun. 1917 — *Fontes*, n. 713; *Acta Apostolicae Sedis*, IX (1917), 305-317.
18. Conc. Trident., sess. V, *de ref.*, c. 2.

at the expense of those who were bound or accustomed to defray the cost.[19]

The Council furthermore ordered the parish priests to explain on all festivals and solemnities, during the solemnization of the Mass or the celebration of the divine office, the divine commands and the maxims of salvation.[20]

The law regarding the days for which the Council of Trent had prescribed preaching remained in force until the Code of Canon Law. The papal constitutions and encyclical letters of the intervening years always insisted on the fulfillment of the obligation of preaching on these particular days.[21]

Moreover, the Sacred Congregation of the Council insisted that pastors were not to be allowed to preach in any other church during Lent with the result of leaving their own parishes in the care of a chaplain.[22] This same Congregation also declared that the pastors were obliged to explain the gospel on feast days, especially during the parochial Mass.[23]

In answer to a query, the Sacred Congregation of the Propagation of the Faith declared that pastors were obliged to preach on Sundays and feast days regardless of the number of parishioners present.[24]

Even though the obligation of preaching in parish churches was definitely established in the decrees of the Council of Trent, it still seemed possible in some quarters to raise the question whether a custom of not preaching could supplant the law of the Council or at least derogate from it. But the Sacred Congregation of the Council denied all abrogative and even derogative force to any contrary usage in this matter.

This is evident from the reply that was given to a certain bishop who had asked whether the usage, as current among pastors in his diocese, of not preaching on feast days of precept when they occurred during the

---

19. Conc. Trident., sess. XXIV, *de ref.*, c. 4.

20. Conc. Trident., sess. XXIV, *de ref.*, c. 7.

21. Innocentius XIII, const. *Apostolici ministerii*, 23 maii 1723, § 11 — *Fontes*, n. 280; Benedictus XIII, const. *Pastoralis officii*, 27 mart. 1726, § 3 — *Fontes*, n. 292; Benedictus XIV, ep. encycl. *Etsi minime*, 7 febr. 1742, § 5 — *Fontes*, n. 324; Pius X, litt. encycl. *Acerbo nimis*, 15 apr. 1905, n. 11; n. 16, I et VI — *Fontes*, n. 666.

22. S.C.C., *Aversana*, 13 febr. 1639 — *Fontes*, n. 2598.

23. S.C.C., *Pientina*, 14 sept. 1748 — *Fontes*, n. 3602.

24. S.C. de Prop. Fide (C.G. — Albaniae), 18 apr. 1757, ad 2 — *Fontes*, n. 4524; *Collectanea . Congregationis de Propaganda Fide* (2 vols., Romae: Typographia Polyglotta, S.C. de Propaganda Fide, 1907), n. 405 (hereafter cited *Collectanea*).

week could be sustained, or whether the pastors were bound to preach on these days as on Sundays; also, whether the pastors could be excused from preaching on the more solemn feast days. The Sacred Congregation answered that the pastors were bound by the law of the Council of Trent to preach on feast days as well as on Sundays. A sustainable contrary custom could not exist, for it was of divine precept that pastors preach to those who are committed to their care.[25] Moreover, such a custom had been expressly reprobated by the Council of Trent itself.[26] However, it was left to the discretion of the ordinary sometimes to dispense from this obligation, namely, when there existed a reasonable cause.[27]

c. The Subject Matter of Preaching

The Council of Trent in its decrees also expressed the subject matter for preaching. It not only declared that parish priests were to announce the Sacred Scriptures and to deliver homilies, but it also expressly ordered that the parish priests give instructions on the commandments of God, on the efficacy and necessity of the sacraments, in fine, on all matters of Christian doctrine.[28] As an aid for the instructions, the Council issued a catechism.[29]

In general the law as enacted in the Council of Trent in this matter was diligently carried out. However, the question arose whether the pastor was required to deliver a formal sermon, or merely the homily on the gospel.

Fagnanus (1598-1678) held that pastors were not obligated to preach a formal sermon. He drew this conclusion from the difference in the words which the Council of Trent used when it placed the obligation of preaching and instructing on bishops and pastors respectively.[30]

---

25. Conc. Trident., sess. XXIII, *de ref.*, c. 1.

26. Conc. Trident., sess. V, *de ref.*, c. 2: "Neque huius decreti executionem consuetudo . . . . . . impedire valeat, quosque desuper a competenti iudice, qui summarie et sola facti veritate inspecta procedat, cognitum et decisum fuerit."

27. S.C.C., *Burgi S. Domnini*, 1 apr. 1876—*Fontes*, n. 4234; *Acta Sanctae Sedis* (41 vols., Romae, 1865-1908), IX (1876), 465-469.

28. Conc. Trident., sess. V, *de ref.*, c. 2; sess. XXII, *de sacrificio Missae*, c. 8; sess. XXIII, *de ref.*, c. 1; sess. XXIV, *de ref.*, c. 4; c. 7; sess. XXV, *decretum de purgatorio;* sess. XXV, *de invocatione, veneratione, et reliquiis sanctorum, et sacris imaginibus.*

29. Conc. Trident., sess. XXIV, *de ref.*, c. 7.

30. *Commentaria in Quinque Libros Decretalium* (5 vols. in 3, Venetiis, 1709), Lib. I, cap. XV, *de officio ordinarii*, n. 33.

Pignatelli (ca. 1695) stated that bishops indeed, but not pastors, were obliged to preach formal sermons.[31] Hinschius (1835-1898) also claimed that pastors were not bound to preach a formal sermon, not even by Pope Innocent XIII in his constitution *Apostolici ministerii* or by Pope Benedict XIII in his constitution *In supremo.*[32]

However, some particular councils which were held during the centuries following the Council of Trent required pastors to preach a formal sermon. The Provincial Council of Gran, Hungary (1858), decreed that pastors should preach a formal sermon, even during the summer time. Moreover, it declared that the Scriptures should be read to the people on the week days during Lent.[33]

The Provincial Council of Vienna (1858) not only imposed the obligation on pastors to preach a formal sermon during the Mass celebrated with greater solemnity, but also required a short homily on the gospel of the day to be given at all the other Masses on Sundays and feast days.[34]

The Provincial Council of Cologne (1860) decreed that on Sundays and feast days pastors should preach a more lengthy sermon at the last Mass, and homilies on the gospel at all the other Masses. This council further commanded the pastors to hold catechetical instructions for the youth of the parish every Sunday afternoon.[35]

The Provincial Council of Utrecht (1865) likewise demanded that a formal sermon be given at the Mass celebrated in a more solemn manner and an explanation of the gospel or an instruction in the Christian faith at all the other Masses on all Sundays and feast days of precept. When only one priest was assigned in the parish, the sermon or instruction could be alternated from Sunday to Sunday. However, for omitting the sermon or the instruction, the permission of the local ordinary was to be obtained.[36]

The III Plenary Council of Baltimore (1884) declared that a formal sermon should be given during the parochial Mass. In all the other Masses

31. *Consultationes Canonicae,* IV, cons. 206, n. 9.
32. Hinschius, *Das Kirchenrecht,* IV, 476.
33. Tit. V, *De hierarchia,* 6, *De sacris curionibus,* n. 3 — *Acta et Decreta Sacrorum Conciliorum Recentiorum, Collectio Lacensis,* auctoribus Presbyteris S. J. e domo B.V.M. sine labe conceptae ad Lacum (7 vols., Friburgi Brisgoviae: Sumptibus Herder, 1870-1892), V, 48 c (hereafter cited *Coll. Lac.*).
34. Tit. IV, cap. IV. — *Coll. Lac.,* V, 182 a, b.
35. Pars secunda, tit. I, cap. VI — *Coll. Lac.,* V, 342 b.
36. Tit. III, cap. V — *Coll. Lac.,* V, 806 a.

on Sundays and feast days of precept, even during the summer months, the gospel of the day was to be read in the vernacular, and a five-minute instruction was to be given.[37]

Pope Pius X (1903-1914), however, in an encyclical letter issued in 1905 stressed the fact that the Council of Trent not only obligated priests who had the care of souls to preach on Sundays and feast days, but also commanded them to teach and instruct the children in catechism on these days. The Supreme Pontiff then ordered all who had the care of souls to instruct the children in the catechism for an hour every Sunday and feast day throughout the entire year without exception. The Pope further called upon pastors to give catechetical instructions to the people in general. This they were to do frequently at an hour that proved convenient to the people. It should be noted that this instruction called for as something shared with the people in addition to the homily which explained the gospel.[38]

d. Penalties for Negligence in Preaching

The Council of Trent admonished the bishops to employ pastoral solicitude to see that the obligation of preaching was duly fulfilled in the parish churches. Pastors and all others who had the care of souls were, if they proved negligent in this matter, to be warned by the bishop that they comply with the decrees of the Council. If for three months after this warning the pastors continued to neglect this duty, the bishop could constrain them with ecclesiastical censures to comply with this obligation. Moreover, the bishop could, if he found it expedient, declare that a fair remuneration, paid from the revenues of the benefice, be given to the one who took the place of the negligent pastor until the latter came to his senses and personally fulfilled his duty.[39]

Pope Innocent XIII (1721-1724) declared that pastors who were negligent in fulfilling their duty of preaching could by means of ecclesiastical censures be compelled to do so; also other punishments could

37. Tit. VII, cap. I, nn. 214-216 — *Acta et Decreta Concilii Plenarii Baltimorensis Tertii, A.D. MDCCCLXXXIV* (Baltimorae: Typis Joannis Murphy et Sociorum, 1886), pp. 115-118 (hereafter cited *Acta et Decreta Balt. III*).

38. Pius X, litt. encycl. *Acerbo nimis*, 15 apr. 1905, n. 11; n. 16, I et VI — *Fontes*, n. 666.

39. Conc. Trident., sess. V, *de ref.*, c. 2.

be inflicted within the discretion of the bishop.[40] Giraldi (1692-1775) taught that the bishop could not employ pecuniary punishments or fines with a view to compelling the negligent pastors to perform their duty.[41] One bishop in his synodal laws had ruled that pastors negligent in preaching could be fined. This statute however was declared void.[42]

The Provincial Council of Paris (1849) suspended the pastors who failed to preach on thirteen consecutive or intermittent Sundays or feast days throughout the year.[43]

The III Plenary Council of Baltimore decreed that those pastors who continued obstinately neglectful in the performance of this duty were to be punished severely by the ordinary.[44]

Finally, the Sacred Consistorial Congregation placed the neglect of explaining the gospel and the catechism among the causes for which a pastor could administratively be removed from his office.[45]

ARTICLE 2.

The Obligation of Preaching on the Part of Regulars and Other Religious

As indicated in the preceding chapter, preaching was a privilege extended to the Friars and to the members of other Religious Orders. Preaching was accordingly not imposed upon them in the nature of an obligation.

But for the convenience of the people, churches which were connected with monasteries or religious houses often acquired the care of souls. The regulars or religious who were elected or presented by their Order or institute to care for the souls of such churches had to submit to an examination relative to their fitness, and then received the approval of the local ordinary as the *vicarii curati* or rectors of such churches.[46]

After such an examination and approval from the ordinary, the regular or religious rector acquired the same prerogatives and contracted

40. Innocentius XIII, const. *Apostolici ministerii*, 23 maii, 1723 — *Fontes*, n. 280.
41. S.C.C., 17 iun. 1658 — Giraldi, *Expositio Iuris Pontificii* (2 vols., Romae, 1829-1830), Pars II, sect. VIII, p. 816.
42. Benedictus XIV, *De Synodo Dioecesana* (2 vols., Romae, 1806), Lib. X, cap. IX, n. 8.
43. Tit. II, cap. IV — *Coll. Lac.*, IV, 22.
44. *Acta et Decreta Balt. III*, n. 216, p. 118.
45. S.C. Consist., decr. *Maxima cura*, 20 aug. 1910, can. 1, n. 8 — *Fontes*, n. 2074.
46. Conc. Trident., sess. VII, *de ref.*, c. 13; sess. XXIV, *de ref.*, c. 18; sess. XXV, *de regularibus*, c. 11.

the same duties that were attached to the pastors of parochial churches. Therefore the same obligation of preaching as incumbent on the pastor extended also to the regular or religious rector of that church to which was attached the care of souls. Consequently he had the obligation of preaching on Sunday and on feast days of precept, and of instructing the children in the catechism.[47] Such a regular or religious rector, when he preached in his own church, needed neither the permission of his superior nor the blessing of the bishop.[48] Moreover, a church thus united to a monastery or religious house was subject to the visitation of the bishop. He was to see that the care of souls was faithfully executed.[49]

The regular or religious rector, like the pastor, had the right to appoint a substitute to take his place in preaching when he was hindered. This substitute however needed the approval of the ordinary.[50]

Furthermore, the regular or religious rector could be punished for his negligence in preaching, the same as the pastor. He could not claim any exemption from such punishment.[51]

Fagnanus declared that a bishop could compel another regular or religious of the same Order to preach in a parish church which was united to the monastery, notwithstanding the fact that sermons were being preached in the monastery church.[52]

Those parish churches which were subject to a monastery or religious house which existed outside of a diocese were to be provided for by the abbot or regular prelate. Any negligence with regard to preaching in such cases was to be reported to the Metropolitan in whose district the house or monastery was situated. The Metropolitan was then to act in the name of the Holy See to enforce the fulfillment of the Council's decrees.[53]

Usually each monastery or religious house had its own church or oratory. Did there exist any obligation of preaching in these churches

47. Conc. Trident., sess. V, *de ref.*, c. 2; sess. XXIV, *de ref.*, cc. 4, 7.

48. S.C.C., *Narnien.*, 13 iul. 1669 — Ojetti, *Synopsis Rerum Moralium et Iuris Pontificii* (3 vols. et Index, Romae, 1909-1914), s. v. *Concionari*, n. 1398.

49. Conc. Trident., sess. XXI, *de ref.*, c. 8; sess. XXV, *de regularibus*, c. 11.

50. Conc. Trident., sess V, *de ref.*, c. 2.

51. Conc. Trident., sess. V, *de ref.*, c. 2.

52. Fagnanus, *Commentaria in Quinque Libros Decretalium*, Lib. I, cap. XV, *de officio ordinarii*, n. 33.

53. Conc. Trident., sess. V, *de ref.*, c. 2.

or oratories? The Council of Trent did not seem to impose any such obligation. But since the privilege of preaching had formerly been granted to the regulars and religious, the Council of Trent did determine the regulations by which one had to abide if he desired to preach in such a church. Here the Council followed a ruling similar to the one given by Pope Leo X in the V General Council of the Lateran. The Council of Trent thus decreed that no regular or religious could preach in a church of his own Order unless he had been examined by his superior concerning his life, morals and knowledge, and then been approved by his superior; moreover, such a regular or religious had then to present himself personally before the bishop and receive the blessing from the bishop before he could preach.[54] The regulars or religious needed also the permission and blessing of the bishop for preaching in churches other than those of their Order.[55]

According to the Council of Trent the regular or religious had to present himself to the bishop personally, and not through letters or a third person, in order to receive the blessing or approval of the bishop as the case might demand. However, because of a possible great distance from the episcopal see and the difficulties attendant upon a long journey, it was made allowable for the bishop to deputize someone who was nearby to grant the blessing or approval in his name.[56] Still later the bishops were admonished to grant this approbation or blessing by means of a letter or through their rural deans.[57]

If the bishop doubted the fitness of a regular or a religious who wished to preach in a church outside his Order he had the right to examine the regular or religious to determine his capability.[58] The bishop was not allowed to deny permission to a capable and approved regular or religious except for a legitimate and reasonable cause. Moreover, he could not deny permission to the entire Order or religious community to

---

54. Conc. Trident., sess. V, *de ref.*, c. 2.

55. Conc. Trident., sess. V, *de ref.*, c. 2.

56. S.C. Ep. et Reg., 20 sept. 1583 — Pignatelli, *Consultationes Canonicae*, IV, cons. 206, n. 67.

57. S.C.C., 10 maii 1635 — Pignatelli, *loc. cit.*

58. S.C.C., *Ugentin.*, 22 ian. 1628 — Ferraris, *Bibliotheca*, s. v. *Praedicare*, n. 66; Clemens X, const. *Superna*, 21 iun. 1670, § § 1, 3 — *Fontes*, n. 246.

preach.[59] The bishop, however, was not obliged to reveal his reason for refusing permission to an individual to preach.[60]

Besides the Council of Trent, later Popes also decreed that the approved regular or religious, if he wished to preach in a church of his own Order, needed the blessing of the local ordinary.[61] The regular or religious was therefore allowed to preach as long as he had sought the blessing of the ordinary, even though it was not granted. But if the blessing was expressly denied, then the regular or religious was not to preach.[62] This blessing was necessary also when the regular or religious preached behind closed doors, or to nuns subject to the Order.[63] If however the regular or religious preached a series of sermons, then it was sufficient for him to obtain the blessing at the beginning of the series. The blessing did not have to be sought before each sermon.[64]

The Sacred Congregation of the Council held that the decretal *Dudum*[65] in the Clementine collection still continued in force. It therefore declared that regulars or religious were not to preach in their own churches when the bishop himself preached or had others solemnly to preach in his presence.[66] However, in a later decree it was stated that the regulars or religious were not to preach in their own churches only when the bishop himself preached. Pastors and also the regular or religious rectors could preach at the principal Mass even though it was being celebrated at the same time that the bishop preached.[67] Notwithstanding this rule the bishops, and in their absence their vicars general, could under

59. S.C. Ep. et Reg., *Salernitana,* 19 nov. 1610 — Pignatelli, *Consultationes Canonicae,* IV, cons. 206, n. 64; Clemens X, const. *Superna,* 21 iun. 1670, § § 1, 3 — *Fontes,* n. 246.

60. S.C.C., *Mediolanen.,* mense iun. 1587, ad VI — *Fontes,* n. 2180.

61. Gregorius XV, const. *Inscrutabili,* 5 febr. 1622, § § 3, 6 — *Fontes,* n. 199; Innocentius X, const. *Cum sicut,* 14 maii 1648, § 3 — *Fontes,* n. 232.

62. Clemens X, const. *Superna,* 21 iun. 1670, § § 1, 3 — *Fontes,* n. 246; S.C.C., *Aquinaten.,* mense dec. 1587 — *Fontes,* n. 2190; S.C.C., *Andrien.,* 23 ian. 1608 — *Fontes,* n. 2369. Cf. also Ferraris, *Bibliotheca,* s. v. *Praedicare,* nn. 71-72; Reiffenstuel, *Ius Canonicum Universum* (7 vols., Parisiis, 1864-1870), Lib. I, tit. 31, nn. 146-147.

63. Clemens X, const. *Superna,* 21 iun. 1670, § § 1, 3—Fontes, n. 246; Feraris, *Bibliotheca,* s.v. *Praedicare,* n. 74.

64. Ferraris, *Bibliotheca,* s.v. *Praedicare,* n. 77.

65. C. 2, *de sepulturis,* III, 7, in Clem.

66. S.C.C., *Pacen.,* 26 apr. 1607 — *Fontes,* n. 2365; S.C.C., *Adiacen.,* 15 mart. 1625 — *Fontes,* n. 2458; S.C.C., *Bituntina,* 17 febr., 2 mart. 1629 — *Fontes,* n. 2504.

67. S.C.C., *Torcellen.,* 21 iun. 1631 — *Fontes,* n. 2532.

the pain of censure forbid the preaching of regulars and religious at the same time that they preached.[68] But bishops were admonished not to forbid such preaching except for a reasonable cause.[69] The Sacred Congregation of the Council also declared that a regular or religious needed to have the approval and blessing of the bishop in each single diocese in which he desired to preach.[70]

The Council of Trent did not determine any punishment for those regulars or religious who preached in their own or other churches without the bishop's approval or blessing. But if they preached heresies, the bishop was not only to forbid them to preach, but he was also to proceed against them in accordance with the requirement of the law or the custom of the locality. The bishop, however, was not to permit a regular or religious to preach at any time if he did not observe residence in a monastery or religious house. Likewise, the bishops was not to allow the seekers of alms to preach.[71]

Popes Gregory XV (1621-1623), Clement X (1670-1676) and Benedict XIV (1740-1758) all declared that the bishop had the right to proceed against delinquent regulars and religious who preached without approbation or blessing. For enforcing this right he could employ censures and other ecclesiastical penalties.[72] The Sacred Congregation of the Council, however, admonished bishops not to abuse their right of suspending regular or religious preachers.[73]

Certainly a regular or a religious sinned gravely in preaching without the approbation or blessing of the bishop. Hollweck (1854-1926) taught that those who preached without this canonical mission incurred an irregularity.[74] Hofmann (+1944), in a review of this work of Hollweck, declared that such regulars or religious who preached without the appro-

68. S.C.C., *Nullius*, 21 iul. 1640, ad 2, 3 — *Fontes*, n. 2619; S.C.C., *Brundusina*, 18 mart. 1645 — *Fontes*, n. 2655; S.C.C., *Urbinaten.*, 3 febr. 1652 — *Fontes*, n. 2718.

69. S.C. Ep. et Reg., *Zagabrien.*, 14 dec. 1674 — *Fontes*, n. 1809.

70. S.C.C., *Bracharen.*, 24 maii 1601, ad 2 — *Fontes*, n. 2338; S.C.C., *Bituntina*, 14 nov. 1626, ad 1 — *Fontes*, n. 2473; S.C.C., *Mechlinien.*, 13 febr. 1639 — *Fontes*, n. 2600.

71. Conc. Trident., sess. V, *de ref.*, c. 2.

72. Gregorius XV, const. *Inscrutabili*, 5 febr. 1622, § § 3, 6 — *Fontes*, n. 199; Clemens X, const. *Superna*, 21 iun. 1670, § § 1, 3 — *Fontes*, n. 246; Benedictus XIV, const. *Ad militantis*, 30 mart. 1742, § 18 — *Fontes*, n. 326.

73. S.C.C., *Belgii*, 23 aug. 1636 — *Fontes*, n. 2584.

74. Hollweck, *Die kirchlichen Strafgesetze* (Mainz, 1899), § 262, n. 3.

bation of the bishop did indeed sin gravely, but they did not incur any irregularity, since their preaching derived from the power of jursdiction, and not from the power of orders. An irregularity was incurred only when one exercised an order which one did not possess; it was not incurred when one exercised an act of jurisdiction which one lacked.[75]

75. Hofmann, "Recensionen," — *Zeitschrift fuer katholische Theologie* (Innsbruck, 1877), XXIII (1899), 703.

PART TWO

CANONICAL COMMENTARY

CHAPTER IV

THE CANONICAL MISSION OR COMMISSION

ARTICLE 1. *The Necessity of the Canonical Mission*

In establishing the Catholic Church, Christ gave to it the characteristics of a completely self-contained society, independent of every other kind of society. The authority residing in the Catholic Church as an autonomous society is bipartite, deriving namely from the power of orders and the power of jurisdiction. The power of orders, received in the Sacrament of Holy Orders, effects the recipient's incorporation in the hierarchy whereby he obtains the right to perform sacred functions. The purpose of this power of orders is the sanctification of the members of the Church.

The power of jurisdiction, on the other hand, accords the right of teaching, guiding and ruling the members of the Church. This power of jurisdiction is also twofold, consisting in the actual and physical governing power, and in the moral and intellectual guidance and teaching faculty. As it pertains to the latter, it is embodied in what is called the ecclesiastical magisterium. The magisterium of the Church, then, may be defined as that part of the ecclesiastical jurisdiction which serves for the dissemination, the preservation and the defense of the Catholic faith.[1]

The means particularly used for obtaining the end of the magisterium are the infallible definitions and declarations of the divinely revealed truths, the preaching of the word of God, and the teaching of these truths in the different grades of schools. It cannot be denied that preaching in a special way pertains to the dissemination of the faith.

But Christ left this infallible magisterium in the hands of St. Peter and the college of the Apostles, to be exercised by them and by their lawful successors. Wherefore, no one is able to exercise this authority of the magisterium unless he be initiated and admitted into the body of

---

1. Moersdorf, *Die Rechtssprache des Codex Iuris Canonici* (Paderborn: Verlag Ferdinand Schoeningh, 1937), p. 249; Wernz, *Ius Decretalium*, Lib. III, tit. II, nn. 26-28.

such authoritative teachers, or unless he be legitimately deputized by such a teacher.[2]

Consequently, canon 1328 of the Code of Canon Law reads:

> Nemini ministerium praedicatonis licet exercere, nisi a legitimo Superiore missionem receperit, facultate peculiariter data, vel officio collato, cui ex sacris canonibus praedicandi munus inhaeret.

It is evident from the canon here quoted that the canonical mission is necessary before one can preach. This is discernible also from the very nature of the infallible magisterium. Moreover, the necessity of the canonical mission for preaching was authentically determined by the Council of Trent.[3] It has been the constant practice of the Church to insist on the indispensability of the canonical mission for preaching.[4] And today the Church is more vigorously insistent on the necessity of the canonical mission to preach in its relationships with civil governments, in order to insure and protect its rights and principles as a sovereign autonomous society.[5]

The word *praedicatio* in canon 1328 is not understood simply in the sense of publicly teaching the salutary truths of the faith, but rather in the strict sense of being the ministry committed by Our Lord Jesus Christ to the Apostles, when He said: "As the father has sent me, I also send you,"[6] "all power is given to me in heaven and on earth,"[7] "go therefore into the whole world and preach the gospel to every creature."[8] Therefore preaching is the exercise of that apostolic office enjoined by Christ and intended directly and immediately to obtain the acceptance of the divine truths of the faith, love for the faith and the supernatual virtues, and the steadfast practice thereof.[9]

---

2. Wernz, *Ius Decretalium,* Lib. III, tit. II, nn. 26-28.
3. Conc. Trident., sess. XXIII, can. 7; sess. V, *de ref.*, c. 1: sess. XXIV, *de ref.*, c. 4.
4. Cf. chapter II of this work.
5. Wernz-Vidal, *Ius Canonicum* (7 vols. in 8, Romae: Apud Aedes Universitatis Gregorianae, 1923-1938), IV, Pars II, 29-30.
6. John, XX:21.
7. Matth., XXVIII:18.
8. Mark, XVI:15.
9. Blat, *Commentarium Textus Codicis Iuris Canonici* (5 vols. in 6), Lib. III, partes II-IV (2. ed., Romae: Ex Typographia Pontificia in Instituto Pii X, 1934), 247-248 (hereafter cited *Commentarium*).

On the other hand, it is doubtful whether the ordinary teaching of the sacred truths, as it is given in schools, requires the canonical mission. Such authors as Coronata,[10] De Meester,[11] Haring (1867,1945),[12] Saegmueller (1860-1942),[13] and Hellmuth[14] have contended that the canonical mission is necessary for catechetical instructions. Jansen is of the same opinion.[15]

The canonical mission appears necessary for catechetical instructions only when one gives such instructions publicly, as in the church, and in place of a sermon, since only under such conditions is one partaking in the apostolic ministry of preaching. The Code of Canon Law does not require the canonical mission in the canons which treat of catechetical instructions. One could indeed argue that since canon 1328 is of a general nature and is placed at the beginning of the title, it is understood to be necessary also for catechetical instructions. But, if it were necessary, it seems that it would be expressly stated, as is done in canon 1337, which requires the canonical mission for sermon preaching.

Moreover, the law does not require the professors in the seminaries to have the canonical mission or the faculties of the diocese.[16] Furthermore, whether one could understand the canonical mission under the words *ius approbandi* in canon 1381, § 3, which gives the right to ordinaries to approve the teachers of religion and the religion books, is again doubtful. In view, however, of the juxtaposition of the words *teachers* and *books*, it hardly seems possible that the canonical mission is meant.

It is also a fact that the teachers in such cases very often are laymen or laywomen; it is impossible that ecclesiastical jurisdiction be granted to them. It is not denied that such teachers should have the approval of

10. *Institutiones Iuris Canonici* (ed. altera, 5 vols., Taurini: Marietti, 1939-1946), II, 251, nota 8 (hereafter cited *Institutiones*).

11. *Juris Canonici et Juris Canonico-civilis Compendium* (nova editio, 3 vols. in 4, Brugis: Desclee de Brouwer, 1921-1928), III, Pars I, 193 (hereafter cited *Compendium*).

12. *Grundzuege des Katholischen Kirchenrechtes* (2 vols., Graz: Ulrich Mosers Buchandlung, 1924), II, 343, nota 4 (hereafter cited *Grundzuege*).

13. *Lehrbuch des katholischen Kirchenrechts* (3 vols. in 1, Breisgau: Herder, 1900-1904), p. 403 (hereafter cited *Lehrbuch*).

14. Hellmuth, "Die Missio Canonica," *Archiv fuer katholisches Kirchenrecht* (Innsbruck, 1857-1861; Mainz, 1862 —), XCI (1911), 450-476.

15. Jansen, *Canonical Provisions for Catechetical Instruction*, The Catholic University of America Canon Law Studies, n. 107 (Washington, D. C.: The Catholic University of America, 1937), pp. 40-44.

16. Cf. cans. 1366, 1367.

the proper ecclesiastical superior, but the canonical mission is not necessary. They may be considered as aids, e. g. to the pastor, and may be classed similarly as those laymen who serve as acolytes at Mass despite their non-reception of any sacred order.[17]

The Sisters or the laity who teach religion in the parochial schools, or in the Catholic high schools and colleges, are not required by law to receive the canonical mission. Likewise, those of the laity who partake in the work of the Confraternity of Christian Doctrine or of Catholic Action groups are not required to, and in fact juridically cannot, receive the canonical mission.

ARTICLE 2. *The Nature of the Canonical Mission*

Since the canonical mission is indispensable for preaching, it seems proper to consider the nature of the canonical mission. In what does it consist? The canonical mission is the positive deputation of one by the competent ecclesiastical authority to teach the Christian faith officially and in a public manner; it consists in the act of ecclesiastical authority by which one is approved and deputized for the exercise of his faculty to preach. It is however different from the authentic testimony of one's capability to preach.[18]

The writer distinguishes the jurisdiction or faculty for preaching according to the manner in which it is granted. If this jurisdiction is attached to the office, it is called the canonical mission; if, however, it is not attached to the office, but is especially granted, it is called the canonical commission. The former connotes ordinary power; the latter, delegated power.[19] In the following article the delegation of that power will be discussed.

Actually, the granting of the canonical mission and commission implies two separate juridical acts: the approbation of the preacher, and the formal deputation. The approbation is the basis for the juridic deputation.

According to canon 1340, § 1, the local ordinaries and religious superiors are bound by a grave obligation in conscience not to grant the

17. Regatillo, *Institutiones Iuris Canonici* (2 vols., Vol. I, 1946; Vol. II, 1942, Santander: Sal Terrae), II, 87 (hereafter cited *Institutiones*).

18. De Meester, *Compendium*, III, Pars I, 193-194.

19. Cf. can. 197, § 1.

faculty or permission of preaching to anyone unless they have satisfied themselves of the candidate's intellectual and moral qualifications by means of an examination according to the norm of canon 877, § 1.

The Norms for Sacred Preaching, as issued by the Sacred Consistorial Congregation, give the manner in which this examination is to be conducted.[20] They require the candidate to undergo an oral and written examination concerning the knowledge and action or delivery before three examiners, who may be chosen at the discretion of the ordinary or religious superior from among the synodal examiners or any of the other clergy. After the candidate's fitness has been adjudged in such a manner, then the local ordinary or religious superior himself should consider with even greater care the candidate's worthiness as regards piety, purity of life and reputation. If this twofold examination leads to satisfactory results, the candidate can be approved as having the necessary qualifications, and only thereupon is the candidate to be deputized by the ordinary or religious superior in the clerical exempt religious institute.

Such examinations, however, are not of strict obligation. If the ordinary has certain knowledge of the candidate's qualifications from other sources, he may deputize the candidate without a previous examination.[21]

To be entirely distinguished from the approbation and deputation are the permission (*licentia*) and consent (*assensus*) required for those who are delegated to preach. Permission of the superior is required when the preacher is competent, that is, has received the canonical commission, but is prohibited from using the faculty licitly because the preacher himself is subject to the superior[22] or desires to exercise the faculty of preaching to persons who are subject to such a superior.[23] Consent is needed for a competent preacher when he is subject to a superior who has only dominative power, or when he preaches to those who are subject to such a superior's dominative power.[24]

---

20. S.C. Consist., *Ut quae,* 28 iun. 1917 — *AAS,* IX (1917), 328; Bouscaren, *The Canon Law Digest* (2 vols., Milwaukee: Bruce, 1934-1943), I, 623-630. It will be noted that these *Norms* were issued shortly before the promulgation of the Code of Canon Law. However, these *Norms* still remain in effect. Only where these is a difference, does the Code prevail.

21. S.C. Consist., *Ut quae,* 28 iun. 1917, nn. 14-16 — Bouscaren, *The Canon Law Digest,* I, 626.

22. Cf. can. 1339, § 2.

23. Cf. cans. 1338, § 2; 1339, § 2.

24. Cf. cans. 1338, § 3; 451, § 1.

The word *permission,* however, is not used uniformly in the Code of Canon Law. In canon 1341 the permission also seems to include the canonical commission.[25]

Just as the delegation of jurisdiction in general can be restricted,[26] so the canonical commission can be restricted, so that the exercise of the faculty of preaching is then permitted only to certain groups or at certain times.[27]

Even though canon 1343, § 2, allows the ordinary to forbid sermon preaching under certain conditions, pastors may nevertheless preach.[28]

Moreover, the delegation of the canonical commission to preach can be revoked. It must be revoked when the preacher has been found to be unworthy and lacking the necessary qualifications. If any doubt should arise, it should be obviated by means of another examination.[29]

Upon revocation of the canonical commission one may have recourse, but without any suspensive effect.[30] The *raison d'etre* of recourse is the deprecatory implications that may be attached to the reputation of the person concerned. Recourse will be made to the Sacred Congregation of the Council, the Sacred Congregation of the Religious, or the Sacred Congregation of the Propagation of the Faith, as the case may demand.[31]

Should one be refused the canonical commission upon first application, there is no explicit provision in the law for recourse. From this, however, it does not follow that the ordinary can indiscriminately and without any solid reason refuse to grant the canonical commission.[32] Thus recourse can always be invoked even though it is not expressly stated in the law.

ARTICLE 3. *The Delegation of the Canonical Commission*

According to canonical principles, one must possess ordinary jurisdiction before one can delegate it. It is, however, allowable for one to subdelegate a delegated jurisdiction, but only when the law grants such

25. Cf. cans. 1341; 1338; 1339; Coronata, *Institutiones,* III, 259, nota 2; III, 265, nota 6.
26. Can. 199, § 1.
27. S.C. Consist., *Ut quae,* 28 iun. 1917, n. 3—Bouscaren, *The Canon Law Digest,* I, 623.
28. S.C.C., *Torcellen.,* 21 iun. 1631—*Fontes,* n. 2532.
29. Can. 1340, § 2.
30. Can. 1340, § 3.
31. Cans. 250, 251, 252.
32. Can. 1339, § 1.

power of subdelegation. Since the local ordinary has by law the care of souls for the entire population of his diocese, it is particularly he who can delegate the faculty of preaching to others. This is evident from the rubric of the eighth Title of the second Book of the Code: "*De potestate episcopali deque iis qui de eadem potestate participant.*" Therefore all others in a diocese partake of the episcopal powers in ruling and teaching the Church.

Some of these partake in this episcopal power in such a manner that the law itself attaches to the particular ecclesiastical office a sharing in the episcopal jurisdiction. Such are the offices of the pastor and of the canon theologian. If, then, the law joins this participation in the ecclesiastical authority to the office, it is called ordinary power. All others who share in this ecclesiastical jurisdiction do so through a special act of delegation on the part of the one who has ordinary power. Thus canon 1337 states:

> Tum clericis e clero saeculari, tum religiosis non exemptis facultas concionandi pro suo territorio solus concedit loci Ordinarius.

The words of the canon, *only the local ordinary*, intend to exclude any other authority, whether civil or ecclesiastical. Hence pastors and canons theologians, even though they possess ordinary power to preach, can not delegate this power. Of course the bishop can grant this right to his priests, especially to the rural deans. In such instances wherein corporations, municipalities or other moral personalities may seem to grant the faculty of preaching, it is to be understood that they have only the right to present or choose the candidate for preaching; the residential bishop alone has the right to approve and depute the candidate.

Moreover, the words, *only the ordinary can concede the jurisdiction*, determine that the delegation of the ordinary is sufficient, and that one does not need the approbation of any other authority. However, these words are not exclusive in the sense that they intend to exclude the power of the Roman Pontiff and his delegates; nor do they intend to exclude the power of the vicar general.[33]

It will be noted that canon 1337 speaks of non-exempt clerical religious. Immediately thereupon the law considers who in a clerical exempt religious institute can delegate the canonical commission. Here the law of the Code differs from the earlier law. Formerly the clerical

---

33. Coronata, *Institutiones*, III, 260.

exempt religious could preach in his own churches with the approbation of his own superior and the blessing of the bishop; in other churches, with the bishop's permission. The law, as stated in canon 1338, § 1, now allows the superior of a clerical exempt religious institute, in accordance of course with the specific provisions in the constitutions, to approve and depute a priest, whether he be of the particular religious institute, of another religious institute, or of the secular clergy, to preach solely to the members of the clerical exempt institute and those who day and night reside there for reasons of study, of health or of service, as explained in canon 514. On all other occasions, whenever a clerical exempt religious preaches, whether to nuns who are subject to the Order, or to the laity who are members of a parish, he must obtain the delegation from the residential bishop.

The *Norms for Sacred Preaching* recognize for the regular ordinary the right of delegating the canonical commission.[34] Only the major superiors of a clerical exempt institute come under the term and name of a regular ordinary.[35] The Code, on the other hand, acknowledges for this right of delegating the canonical commission the superior of the clerical exempt institute who is thus designated in the constitutions. It makes no distinction between minor and major superiors. Hence, according to the Code, minor superiors can delegate the canonical commission when the constitutions of the Order or the institute designate him as a properly suited superior for that purpose.

Furthermore, the law requires the regular superior simply to delegate the canonical commission to a qualified and fit preacher outside the Order. Consequently, the regular superior does not seem to have the right to subject the preachers outside of the Order to an examination, in order to determine their qualifications. He should rather accept the testimony of the preacher's superior concerning his qualifications.[36]

Augustine (1872-1943) seemed to imply that the superior of the non-exempt clerical institute has the same right of granting the delegation as the superior of the exempt clerical institute.[37] Canon 1338, § 1, definitely

34. S.C. Consist., *Ut quae*, 28 iun. 1917, n. 18—Bouscaren, *The Canon Law Digest*, I, 626.

35. Cans. 488, 8°; 198, § 1.

36. Blat, *Commentarium*, Lib. III, partes II-IV, 262.

37. Augustine, *A Commentary on the New Code of Canon Law* (3. ed., 8 vols., St. Louis, Mo.: B. Herder Book Co., 1919-1931), VI, 353 (hereafter cited *A Commentary*).

excludes such a right of the superior of a non-exempt clerical institute, since it speaks precisely of the exempt clerical superior. Moreover, the preceding canon expressly mentions that non-exempt clerical religious must obtain the delegation from the local ordinary. This is also apparent from the very nature of the non-exempt clerical institute.[38]

The local ordinary alone can grant the faculty to preach whenever the sermon is delivered before lay religious, whether men or women, exempt or non-exempt.[39] This therefore excludes the superior of such an institute. It also excludes the right of the pastor to delegate the faculty of preaching to members of such an institute even though the institute is within the boundaries of his parish.

The faculty to preach is granted territorially; hence outside the territory for which the faculty was granted no one can lawfully make use of the faculty. Consequently the law requires the permission of the local ordinary before an extradiocesan priest can be invited to preach. Although the word *permission* is used in this canon, it is understood to mean also the faculty to preach. This is clear from the general laws of canon 1337 and n. 5 of the *Norms*.[40]

The ordinary should not allow an extradiocesan priest to preach unless he is certain of the candidate's qualifications. Testimony of the extradiocesan's qualifications should be obtained from his own ordinary or superior, who when questioned must answer truthfully.[41] According to the testimony received, the ordinary may either grant or deny the permission and the faculty to preach, accountable only to God regarding the reason for the refusal.[42]

Hence this permission must be obtained in due time before the actual date of the preaching. *In due time* has been declared to mean two months.[43] However, since communication is swifter nowadays, the time can be left to the prudent judgment of the petitioner, as long as it has not been delayed purposely, so that the ordinary would not be able to

38. Berutti, *Institutiones Iuris Canonici* (6 vols., Vol. IV, Taurini, Romae: Marietti, 1940), IV, 349 (hereafter cited *Institutiones*); Schaefer, *De Religiosis ad Norman Codicis Iuris Canonici* (3. ed. aucta et emendata, Roma: Herder, 1940), pp. 222, 867 (hereafter cited *De Religosis*).

39. Can. 1338, § 3.

40. Berutti, *Institutiones*, IV, 353-354.

41. Can. 1341, § 1.

42. S.C. Consist., *Ut quae*, 28 iun. 1917, n. 12—Bouscaren, *The Canon Law Digest*, I, 625.

43. S.C.C., *Theatinen.*, 19 apr. 1728, 30 apr. 1729—*Fontes*, n. 3340.

ascertain the qualifications of the preacher. If, on the other hand, the ordinary has determined the time within which such a request must be made, this regulation must be followed.

This permission is to be obtained by the pastor, if the church in question is a parochial church; by the rector, if the church is not subject to the pastor; by the first dignitary with the consent of the chapter, if it is a capitular church;[44] by the director or chaplain of the confraternity, if the church belongs to the confraternity; by the competent religious superior, if it is a religious church or oratory; by the one who has the right to perform the sacred functions, if it is a church or oratory of Sisters; by the one who has the right to perform the sacred functions according to canons 415 and 698, if it is a church which is a parish church and at the same time has a chapter or belongs to a confraternity.[45] The permission of the ordinary should be given in writing, designating the place and the kind of preaching for which it is granted. It is understood that the faculty to preach is given at the same time as the permission.[46]

Pruemmer (1866-1931) felt that these regulations are binding only when there is question of sermons to be delivered on the more solemn or rare occasions, for otherwise the priest would have to contend with too much of a burden when he invites an extradiocesan for giving the ordinary and usual sermons.[47] Vermeersch (1858-1936)-Creusen and Cocchi supported the same opinion.[48]

The writer does not sustain this opinion. Certainly the extradiocesan priest lacks the canonical commission for preaching outside of his own diocese. He therefore would preach unlawfully, and both he and the priest who invited him would be liable to punishment. This case often presents itself to the priest who, being outside of his own diocese on vacation, may be asked by his host on Sunday to preach at one of the Masses. The justification for accepting the invitation in such a

---

44. The Code requires the consent of the chapter, while the *Norms* speak of consulting the chapter. The Code prevails. The consent is necessary.

45. Cocchi, *Commentarium In Codicem Iuris Canonici* (8 vols. in 5, Vol. VI, 3. ed., Taurini: Marietti, 1933), VI, 55 (hereafter cited *Commentarium*).

46. S.C. Consist., *Ut quae,* 28 iun. 1917, n. 9—Bouscaren, *The Canon Law Digest*, I, 625.

47. *Manuale Iuris Canonici* (6. ed., Friburgi Brisgoviae: Herder, 1933), q. 405, 4, pp. 485-486.

48. Vermeersch-Creusen, *Epitome Iuris Canonici* (6. ed., 3 vols., Romae: Dessain, 1937-1946), II, n. 676 (hereafter cited *Epitome*); Cocchi, *Commentarium,* VI, 56.

case as presented by MacCarthy,[49] on the score that the invitation was not of a formal character and that the use of epikeia is in place, does not seem properly warranted. The whole tenor of the law and of the *Norms* seems to militate against abuses and errors in preaching, and to aim at insuring fruitful sermon preaching. In practice, however, many ordinaries do grant to their priests the right to invite an extradiocesan preacher under the condition that they ascertain the preacher's qualifications.[50]

Attention is called here to the privilege which by law is granted to Cardinals. They can preach the word of God everywhere.[51] Also bishops, whether residential or titular, have the privilege by law to preach the word of God everywhere, but with the presumed permission (consent) of the local ordinary.[52]

Sacred Orders, that is, priesthood and deaconship, are prerequisites for the reception of the canonical commission. However, it is the policy at present in the Church that the habitual use of the faculty to preach is not granted to deacons. The ordinary should not delegate other clerics to preach except for a reasonable cause and in particular cases. All laymen, even though they are members of a religious institute, are forbidden to preach in church.[53]

It is allowable for laymen to read prayers, to speak at lay society meetings, and even to teach catechism in church, as long as they do not use the pulpit or the particular place that is set aside for the preaching of the word of God. Such acts are not considered as sermon preaching. Moreover, a superioress of a religious institute may give an exhortation in the semi-public oratory of the religious institute. This procedure seems allowable, since in the strict sense of the word an exhortation is not a sermon.[54]

49. "The New Regulations on Preaching," *The Ecclesiastical Review*, LVII (1917), 383, n. 8.

50. Snee-Clark, "Synthesis of the Diocesan Faculties in the United States," *Theological Studies* (Woodstock, Md., 1940-), IX (1948), 351-375-377.

51. Can. 239, § 1, 3°.

52. Can. 349, § 1, 1°.

53. Can. 1342.

54. Regatillo, *Institutiones*, II, 92.

CHAPTER V

THE OBLIGATION OF PREACHING

ARTICLE 1. *The Source of the Obligation*

Canon 1344, § 1, places an obligation on pastors to preach the customary homily every Sunday and feast day of precept. The common law seems to admit that the obligation of preaching arises from the office of pastor: "*proprium cuiusque parochi officium est . . .*" Does, then, this obligation stem from the office of the pastor, and what is its nature? The authors speak very little of the obligation of preaching even though it is a matter of far-reaching importance. Most of the canonists seem content simply to mention that the obligation arises from the teaching of the Council of Trent. Some few devote a little discussion to the characteristics of this obligation. In order to understand the gravity of this obligation, one must inquire into the source whence it arises.

Since the common law intimates that the office of pastor is the source of the obligation, it is necessary to analyze this office. Canon 451, § 1, describes the office of the pastor:

> Parochus est sacerdos vel persona moralis cui paroecia collata est in titulum cum cura animarum sub Ordinarii loci auctoritate exercenda.

The essential element of the pastorate therefore is the care of souls, which the priest exercises with a participation in ecclesiastical authority.

Bouix (1808-1870) regarded as the constituent and essential elements of the care of souls at least the preaching of the word of God and the administration of the sacraments. By this, however, he did not disclaim other integral parts of the care of souls. He insisted, though, that one cannot be called a pastor, if one is not bound by his office either to preach the word of God, or to administed the sacraments.[1]

Capello,[2] Chelodi (1880-1922),[3] and Pruemmer[4] placed preaching among those obligations which are incumbent on the pastor by reason of

1. *Tractatus de Parocho* (3. ed., Parisiis, 1880), Pars I, sectio II, cap. IX, pp. 170-175.

2. *Summa Iuris Canonici* (3 vols., Vols. I - II, 4. ed., 1945; Vol. III, 2 ed., 1940, Romae: Apud Aedes Universitatis Gregorianae), I, 478 (hereafter cited *Summa*).

3. *Ius Canonicum de Personis* (3. ed. curavit Pius Ciprotti, Vicenza: Societa Anonima Tipografica, 1942), pp. 357-359 (hereafter cited *De Personis*).

4. *Manuale Iuris Canonici,* q. 157, p. 213.

his office, that is, in consequence of the fact that he has the care of souls.

Berardi (1854-1916),[5] Berengo[6] and Bargilliat (1853-1926)[7] claimed that the pastor's obligation of preaching derives from divine precept. They based their arguments on the words of the Council of Trent: "Since by divine precept it is enjoined on all to whom is entrusted the care of souls to know their sheep (John, X:1-16; XXI:15-17; Acts, XX:28), to offer sacrifice for them, and to feed them by the preaching of the divine word, the administration of the sacraments. . . ."[8]

True, the Council of Trent did command all who had the care of souls to preach, and that by divine precept. But these words were primarily directed to the bishops. Moreover, as Bouix remarked, the word "pastor" as used in the juridic language does not have the same significance as this word imports in the language of Sacred Scriptures. In the scriptural sense the word "pastor" connotes not only the duty of feeding the flock, but also of guiding and leading it, of protecting it, and of castigating its errant members. Thus in Sacred Scripture it embraces the notion of the threefold ecclesiastical power, namely, the legislative, the judicial and the coactive.[9] So in the strict sense, comprising the offices of teacher, sanctifier, judge and ruler, the title of pastor really belongs only to the successors of the Apostles. Certainly the pastors, according to the present common law, do not enjoy this threefold authority.

Berengo, moreover, maintained that the office of pastor itself was a divine institution. According to his opinion, the pastors are the successors of the seventy-two dsciples of Christ.[10] He seems to stand alone in his contention for the divine institution of the pastorship.

St. Thomas (1225-1274) already had taught that the office of pastor was an ecclesiastical institution.[11] Berengo no doubt failed to distinguish between the concepts of priest and pastor. The pastor in so far as he is a

---

5. *De Parocho Compendium* (Faventiae: Ex Typographia Novelli, 1887), Pars I, cap. IV, pp. 28-40.

6. *Enchiridion Parochorum seu Institutiones Theologiae Pastoralis* (2. ed., Venetiis, 1877), Pars II, cap. II, n. 56, pp. 89-90 (hereafter cited *Enchiridion Parochorum*).

7. *Praelectiones Juris Canonici* (37. ed., 2 vols., Parisiis: Baston, Berche et Pagis, 1923), II 50, (hereafted cited *Praelectiones*).

8. Conc. Trident., sess. XXIII, *de ref.*, c. 1; cf. Schroeder, *Council of Trent*, p. 164.

9. Bouix, *Tractatus de Parocho*, Pars I, sectio II, cap. VI, pp. 142-145.

10. Berengo, *Enchiridion Parochorum*, Pars I, cap. I, n. 7, pp. 20-22.

11. *Summa Theologica*, Pars IIa-IIae, q. 188, a. 4 ad 5.

priest reflects the divine institution of the sacred orders he has received, but in his office of pastor, that is, as one having the care of souls, he reflects an ecclesiastical institution. Hence no canonist of the present age holds the opinion which Berengo proposed; in fact, many have proved it to be false by demonstrating the contrary.

The office of pastor is not even of divine-apostolic institution. The history of canonical institutes does not reveal anywhere the office of pastor before the fifth century.[12]

On the other hand, the obligation of preaching arises out of the natural law. The fact that a pastor has accepted the care of souls binds him by the natural law to fulfill all the duties which the care of souls requires of him. Coronata,[13] Chelodi,[14] and Pruemmer[15] are content to assert that the pastor is bound in justice to preach.

Cappello teaches that the pastor is bound not only in justice to exercise the care of souls, particularly by preaching, but also by a quasi-contract, entered into through the acceptance of the parochial office. Cappello does not, however, further describe the quasi-contract.[16]

Cocchi, in explaining the title by which the pastor possesses the parish, also claims that this title gives the pastor the right to a congruous sustenance, while the same title obligates him to serve the needs of the parish to which he is assigned.[17]

The quasi-contract of which Cappello and Cocchi speak seems to mean this: when the pastor takes possession of the parish, there exists, as it were, an agreement between the members of the parish and the pastor; on his part, he will give them all the things necessary for the attainment of eternal salvation, while the members, on their part, will support the pastor.[18]

---

12. Wernz, *Ius Decretalium,* Lib. II, tit. XXXIX, n. 820; Koudelka, *Pastors, Their Rights and Duties According to the New Code of Canon Law,* The Catholic University of America Canon Law Studies, n. 11 (Washington, D. C.: The Catholic University of America, 1921), pp. 7-8; Rossi, *De Paroecia iuxta Codicem Iuris Canonici* (Romae: Pustet, 1923), pp. 67-71; Sipos, *Enchiridion Iuris Canonici* (3. ed., Pecs: Ex Typographia "Haladas R.T.," 1936), pp. 308-309; Cocchi, *Commentarium,* III (4. ed. recognita, Taurinorum Augustae: Marietti, 1940), 389.

13. *Institutiones,* I, 579.

14. *De Personis,* pp. 357-359.

15. *Manuale Iuris Canonici,* q. 157, p. 213.

16. *Summa,* I, 478.

17. Cocchi, *Commentarium,* III, 390.

18. Fanfani, *De Iure Parochorum* (Taurini-Romae: Marietti, 1924), p. 3.

It is evident that from this quasi-contract there does not arise any strict commutative justice by which the pastor is bound to fulfill his obligation to preach. He is, however, bound by distributive justice.

Hence the pastor's obligation of preaching has its source in the care of souls in which he by ecclesiastical law participates. Furthermore, this obligation is a grave one, founded in justice, and arising out of the fact that the natural law itself places this obligation upon him once he has accepted the parochial office.

ARTICLE 2. *Characteristics of the Obligation*

From a consideration of canon 1344, it appears that the obligation of preaching has certain characteristics, namely, the obligation is personal, real, temporal and grave.

That the obligation of preaching is personal follows from the nature of the pastoral office as well as from the statement in canon 1344, § 2. The incumbent of a pastoral office is selected by the bishop as the pastor of a particular parish. Inasmuch as he was chosen for his personal qualities, it is he upon whom the obligation of preaching primarily rests.[19]

But, as Cappello states, it is not as strict a personal obligation as that of the *Missa pro populo*.[20] The pastor is bound personally to satisfy this obligation unless he be excused for a just cause. Thus, the personal obligation does not bind everywhere and at all times in such a manner that he never can be excused from the obligation. Cappello demands a legitimate cause for an excuse; the canon, however, demands a just cause. The causes for which the pastor may be excused are many. But they may be included under the headings of absolute or moral impossibility, of legitimate absence, of greater utility for the people, and of the obligation of celebrating the conventual Mass.

This just cause must be approved by the ordinary if there is question of a habitual abstention from preaching on the part of the pastor. The pastor does not have the right to excuse himself in such a case. All the authors, however, admit that the pastor could once or twice omit preaching for a very insignificant cause as long as others preached for him. Moreover, it may be noted that the assistants cannot habitually fulfill this obligation of the pastor unless the permission of the ordinary is ob-

---

19. Augustine, *A Commentary*, VI, 364-365.
20. Cappello, *Summa*, I, 485.

tained.[21] Tanquerey (1854-1932) admitted that the assistants and the pastor may take turns in preaching on the required days.[22]

The law in such a case is not breached if the ordinary has approved of such a practice either in a synod, in a circular letter, or through some other means.[23]

The pastor, however, can presume the approval of the ordinary in extraordinary circumstances. Such extraordinary circumstances may be the sudden illness of the pastor, or his necessary and unexpected departure.[24]

The obligation of preaching, in contradistinction to being personal is also real, that is, if the pastor personally is unable or has been excused from preaching, he nevertheless must provide for a sermon by securing the service of other approved preachers. Both De Meester and Berutti explicitly state that the pastor's obligation to preach is real, and does not cease when he personally cannot fulfill the obligation.[25]

Other authors offer no apodictic proof for the existence of a real obligation. Nevertheless, the real obligation becomes apparent when one considers the importance of the duties which arise from the care of souls. Moreover, there is even a greater necessity for sermon preaching when the parishioners are in need of the word of God. It is a known fact that the Catholic laity of today do not read sufficient Catholic literature on doctrinal or purely religious subjects. Where are they to acquire their knowledge of the faith and an appreciation thereof, if not from the pulpit?[26] Hence there exists a real obligaton of preaching, so that should the pastor personally be excused or indisposed, he has the obligation to secure the services of other preachers.

The obligation of preaching is also of a temporal character, inasmuch as the pastor is required to fulfill this obligation on certain days, namely, on Sundays and on the feast days of precept. The particular hour however is not prescribed by the common law; its selection is left to the

21. Berutti, *Institutiones*, IV, 357.

22. *Synopsis Theologiae Moralis et Pastoralis* (3 vols., Vol I, 11. ed., 1930; Vols. II-III, 9. ed., 1930-1931, Parisiis, Tornaci, Romae: Desclee et Socii), III, 558-559.

23. Augustine, *A Commentary*, VI, 364-366.

24. Berutti, *Institutiones*, IV, 356-357.

25. De Meester, *Compendium*, II, 312; Berutti, *Institutiones*, IV, 356-357.

26. Woywod, *A Practical Commentary on the Code of Canon Law* (9. ed., 2 vols., revised by Rev. Callistus Smith, O.F.M., New York: Joseph F. Wagner, Inc., 1945), II, 100 (hereafter cited *A Practical Commentary*).

prudent judgment of the pastor. The time of preaching will be discussed further in a succeeding chapter.

Finally, the obligation of preaching is grave in its character. All authors agree that the pastor's obligation is a grave one. Yet all authors admit that it is not always a mortal sin to omit the sermon. The authors, however, disagree as to what constitutes a mortal sin of negligence in sermon preaching.

F. Suarez (1548-1617) claimed that the pastor did not sin gravely if he now and then, or even often, omitted the sermon; the Council of Trent did not oblige pastors under such a grave obligation.[27]

St. Alphonsus (1696-1787), Scavini (1790-1869), Bouix (1808-1870), Aertnys (1828-1915)-Damen, Tanquerey, Cappello and Coronata have all asserted that the pastor sins gravely if he omits the sermon for one month continuously or for three months interruptedly in the course of a year. This, they claimed to be the common teaching of the authors.[28]

Barbosa (1589-1649), Ferraris (ca. 1763), and Ballerini (1805-1881) regarded the pastor as sinning gravely only when he omitted the sermon for three months. Ferraris considered it a grave sin if the pastor omitted the sermon for three interrupted months; Ballerini, however, postulated a negligence of three continuous months before the pastor could be charged with grave sin.[29]

Lehmkuhl (1834-1918), on the other hand, claimed that a pastor became gravely guilty when he omitted the sermon continuously somewhat over a month, for example two months. The pastor also sinned gravely if he omitted the sermon somewhat over a period of three interrupted months throughout the year, especially if scandal was thereby

---

27. *Opera Omnia* 28 vols., Parisiis: Apud Ludovicum Vives, 1856-1878), tract. II, lib. II, cap. XVI, n. 7, p. 319.

28. Liguori (St. Alphonsus), *Theologia Moralis* (ed. accuratior, 2 vols., Augustae Taurinorum: Ex Typis Hyacinthi Marietti, 1879), Lib. III, n. 269, pp. 382-383; Scavini, *Theologia Moralis Universa* (11. ed., 4 vols., Mediolani, 1869), I, tract. III, n. 452, p. 348; Bouix, *Tractatus de Parocho,* Pars V. cap. IX, n. 10, p. 590; Aertnys-Damen, *Theologia Moralis* (14. ed., 2 vols., Taurini: Marietti, 1944), I, 804; Tanquerey, *Synopsis Theologiae Moralis et Pastoralis,* III, 558-559; Cappello, *Summa,* I, 487; Coronata, *Institutiones,* II, 271.

29. Barbosa, *De Officio et Potestate Parochi,* Pars I, c. XIV, nn. 7-8; Ferraris, *Bibliotheca,* s.v. *Parochus,* art. II, nn. 71-73; Ballerini-Palmieri, *Opus Theologicum Morale* (7 vols., Prati, 1889-1893), II, tract. VI, sect. IV, *de 4° praecepto Decalogi,* nn. 82-85, pp. 592-593.

given.[30] Vermeersch (1856-1936) cited this opinion of Lehmkuhl with apparent approval, for he did not advert to any divergent doctrine.[31]

Berardi (1854-1916) introduced another element into the consideration of grave negligence on the part of the pastor for not fulfilling the obligation of preaching. Besides the time element, Berardi averred that the circumstances of each particular case needed to be considered. Such circumstances were: whether it was a large or a small parish; whether the pastor was detained by any impediment; whether scandal resulted; whether the parishioners had need of hearing sermons.[32]

E. Suarez follows this line of thought of Berardi. He claims that a pastor who in ordinary circumstances neglects homily on half of the required days throughout the year sins gravely. On the other hand, the pastor who has two parishes, and on alternating Sundays throughout the year delivers the homily in each parish, does not sin gravely. He gives the general rule: the serious gravity of the negligence depends on the prudent judgment of the bishop, as gauged according to the circumstances of the diocese, the region, or the parish, just as long as the negligence can be considered at least as habitual.[33]

What conclusion can be drawn from these many opinions of the authors? First, the common law does not determine what is understood by grave negligence in this matter, neither in canon 2382 nor in canons 2182-2185. It seems the law in this regard has not changed essentially. Consequently, according to canon 6, 2°, the interpretation will be made according to the former law.

The Council of Trent did not specifically determine the gravity of negligence. The Council decreed that, if after being warned the pastor continued to neglect the obligation of preaching for three months, the ordinary should proceed against him with ecclesiastical censures. Thus the Council of Trent certainly considered a continued negligence for three months after a warning as a grave sin, since an ecclesiastical penalty was then to be inflicted. The Council did not determine whether the three months were to be understood as continuous or interrupted. How-

30. *Theologia Moralis* (9. ed., 2 vols., Friburgi Brisgoviae: Herder, 1898-1899), II, lib. I, n. 280, p. 454.

31. *Theologiae Moralis Principia, Responsa, Concilia* (3. ed., 4 vols., Roma: Universita Gregoriana, 1933-1937), III, 83.

32. *De Parocho Compendium,* Pars I, cap. IV, n. 145, p. 39.

33. *De Remotione Parochorum* (Romae: Pontificium Internationale Institutum "Angelicum" de Urbe, 1931), pp. 181-182.

ever, according to the rule of law: *Odia restringi et favores convenit ampliari*,[34] one can say that a negligence for three continuous months was postulated before the canonical punishment could be inflicted.

McVann consequently concludes that a negligence for three continuous months constitutes a grave sin.[35] The writer agrees with McVann that a negligence for three continuous months must have preceded before any penalty ought to be inflicted. However, that does not imply that only a negligence for three continuous months is to be considered as a grave sin. it is not necessary that every mortal sin be punished with an ecclesiastical penalty. In fact, the Code inflicts penalties on very few mortal sins or delicts. To the writer, therefore, there appears no solid reason for receding from the so called common opinion of the authors, according to which it is stated that the pastor sins gravely if with regard to preaching he has been totally negligent for one continuous month or for three months of the year interruptedly.

ARTICLE 3. *The Clerics Who Have the Obligation of Preaching*

Canon 1344, § 1, definitely declares that the pastor has the obligation of preaching. The development of this obligation incumbent on the pastor has been discussed. There remains, however, to determine the time at which this obligation as binding on the pastor becomes operative. The pastor accepts this obligation the moment he takes possession of the parish.[36]

The pastor, after having received the appointment to the pastorate from the ordinary, and making the profession of faith, takes possession of his office through the act of installation. The formal procedure for the act of installation is not determined by the common law; it is left to the special or particular prescriptions of the ordinary or to the regulations deriving from legitimate custom. For a just cause the ordinary can dispense from the formalities of the installation. When such a dispensation is granted, it stands in lieu of the act of taking possession of the office.[37]

---

34. Reg. 15, R. J., in VI°.
35. McVann, *The Canon Law on Sermon Preaching* (New York: The Paulist Press, 1940), p. 109.
36. Fanfani, *De Iure Parochorum*, p. 359.
37. Can. 1444, § 1; Coronata, *Institutiones*, II, 391.

Several authors hold the opinion that, apart from an express dispensation, the corporal installation of the pastor is necessary for the valid and lawful possession of a parish.[38] Schaaf considers a decree of the ordinary in which the date for the beginning of the tenure of office is stated as sufficient for the validity of the corporal installation.[39] If no particular ceremonial for the corporal installation of the pastor is observed, Beste and Park demand that the ordinary give an explicit and written dispensation therefrom; they hold the opinion that the letter of appointment in which the date for accepting the office is determined is not equivalent to a dispensation.[40]

No matter what opinion one may follow in this matter, it is certain that the pastor who does not validly take possession of his parish contracts neither the rights nor the obligations arising therefrom. Hence in such a case, the factual incumbent would not be subject in law to the obligation of preaching.

Quasi-pastors are those priests who have the care of souls in quasi-parishes. The quasi-parish is a canonically designated section of a vicariate apostolic or a prefecture apostolic.[41] The quasi-parish exists only in mission territory. The name is not to be applied to any other determined portion of the faithful.[42] The quasi-pastors, however, are in the common law equivalent to pastors and come under the name of pastors.[43]

Thus the quasi-pastors have the same rights and obligations as pastors, even though they have possession of the quasi-parishes not in title, but by mandate. They are entrusted simply with the administration of the quasi-parishes, also relative to the care of souls.[44] Nevertheless they should

---

38. Beste, *Introductio in Codicem* (3. ed., Collegeville, Minn.: St. John's Abbey Press, 1946), p. 728; Park, "The Necessity of Installation of Pastors," *The Homiletic and Pastoral Review*, XXXV (1934-1935), 579-592 (hereafter abbreviated *HPR*); Coronata, *Institutiones*, II, 391; Bouscaren-Ellis, *Canon Law, A Text and Commentary* (Milwaukee; Bruce Publishing Co., 1946), p. 202 (hereafter cited *Canon Law*).

39. Schaaf, "Corporal Installation of Pastors," *The Ecclesiastical Review*, XCI (1934), 622.

40. Beste, *Introductio in Codicem*, p. 728; Park, "The Necessity of Installation of Pastors," *HPR*, XXXV (1934-1935), 582.

41. Can. 216, § 3.

42. S.C. Consist., declar., 1 aug. 1919—*AAS*, XI (1919), 346.

43. Can. 451, § 2, 1°.

44. Toso, *Ad Codicem Iuris Canonici Commentaria Minora* (5 vols., Vol. I, 2. ed., 1921; Vol. II-V, 1922-1927, Romae: Marietti), IV, 96 (hereafter cited *Commentaria Minora*).

take possession of the quasi-parishes through an act of corporal installation in the same manner as pastors.[45] Since the quasi-pastors have the same rights and obligations in law as the pastors, they also have the obligation of preaching the homily on Sundays and feast days of precept. This obligation arises not only out of charity, but also out of justice, that is, as a strict demand which derives from their office.

Also having the same rights and obligations as pastors are the parochial vicars who are endowed with the full parochial power. Under the general category of parochial vicars the Code names:

a) The actual vicar of a parish held in title by a moral person (can. 471);
b) The parish administrator (can. 472, 1°; can. 473);
c) The curate or assistant lawfully constituted to act as pastor when the parochial office falls vacant (can. 472, 2°);
d) The substitute vicar (can. 465, §§ 4, 5; can. 474; can 1923, § 2);
e) The adjutant vicar (can. 475);
f) The assistant vicar (can. 476).

The obligation of preaching incumbent on each of these vicars will be discussed briefly.

a) The actual vicar is that priest who is placed in charge and has the care of souls of a church which has been united or incorporated with a religious house, a chapter, or some other moral personality. The moral personality is made responsible for the care of souls, but it must constitute an actual vicar who holds the exclusive actual right of exercising the care of souls with all the rights and obligations of a pastor. Hence such an actual vicar, also in the event that he is a religious, has the obligation of preaching.[46]

b) The parish administrator is that priest who is appointed to take the place of the pastor when the parish has become vacant. During the interim, until a new pastor is appointed to fill the vacancy, the administrator contracts the same rights and obligations as the pastor in all things which pertain to the care of souls. Thus the parish administrator likewise has the obligation of preaching.[47]

45. Beste, *Introductio in Codicem*, p. 230.
46. Beste, *Introductio in Codicem*, p. 471.
47. Coronata, *Institutiones*, I, 592; De Meester, *Compendium*, II, 333.

c) According to canon 472, 2°, the assistant vicar is to assume control of the parish immediately upon its vacancy and until the appointment of a parish administrator or of a new pastor. Such an assistant vicar then is given by the law the same rights and obligations as the pastor. He must therefore preach the homily on Sundays and feast days of precept. It will be noted, however, that the assistant vicar is to assume this office along with its obligations and duties only if the ordinary has not by means of diocesan law or through a particular decree made provision in some other manner.[48]

d) The substitute vicar who has been legitimately appointed to take the pastor's place has the same obligations as the pastor relative to the duty of preaching.[49]

e) Whether the adjutant vicar who is appointed to take the place of an incapacitated pastor has or has not the obligation of preaching depends on the reasons for which he was deputed. Ordinarily the letter of appointment will determine his status and specifically define his duties and obligations. If he has been deputed with full parochial powers, he also has the obligation of preaching.[50]

f) The primary obligation of preaching does not devolve on the assistant vicar who is appointed to aid the pastor in the care of souls unless the ordinary has, in his letter of appointment, placed such a specific obligation on the assistant vicar.[51] The assistant vicar can take the pastor's place habitually in delivering the required and customary homily only if there is a just cause which has been sanctioned by the ordinary.[52]

In the case where a parochial vicarage has been erected as a benefice, according to canons 477, § 2, 1409, 1412, 1°, the question may arise whether such a vicar assistant is bound to preach by reason of his office. Even though the care of souls may be attached to such a parochial vicarage, it does not seem that the obligation of preaching the homily

48. Coronata, *Institutiones,* I, 592.

49. Wagner, *Parochial Substitute Vicars and Supplying Priests,* The Catholic University of America Canon Law Studies, n. 265 (Washington, D. C.: The Catholic University of America Press, 1947), pp. 92-93.

50. Can. 475, § 1; De Meester, *Compendium,* II, 337.

51. Can. 476, § 6; De Meester, *Compendium,* II, 346; Pruemmer, *Manuale Iuris Canonici,* q. 152, pp. 207-208.

52. Berutti, *Institutiones,* IV, 357.

and giving the catechetical instructions devolves on the assistant vicar. Canon 1344, § 1, definitely and primarily places the obligation of preaching on the pastor. Moreover such an assistant vicar is subject to the pastor in matters which pertain to the exercise of his functions.[53]

There are other groups of priests who may have the care of souls, such as rectors, chaplains of lay religious houses, chaplains of hospitals, and military chaplains. Do these also have the obligation of preaching? It seems that none of these have the obligation according to the manner determined in canon 1344.

Rectors are those priests who care for a church and celebrate the divine services in a church which is of such a character that it is neither a parochial church, nor a capitular church, nor a church attached to a religious house.[54] Even though some authors hold that rectors have an ecclesiastical office in the strict sense of the word, nevertheless they do not fall within the category of priests contemplated in canon 451, § 2. Consequently they are not equivalent to pastors, nor do they have the same duties and obligations as pastors. Hence they do not have the obligation of preaching after the manner in which this obligation receives mention in canon 1344. The ordinary, however, can demand that such rectors preach on Sundays and feast days of precept.[55]

Chaplains of lay religious houses must receive the delegation for preaching from the local ordinary, even though they may have been appointed by the religious superior. They therefore do not have any strict obligation of preaching unless the local ordinary's act of delegation implies at the same time not only the right but also the duty to exercise the delegated power.[56]

Chaplains of lay societies, of pious unions, of confraternities and the like similarly need the deputation of the local ordinary before they become authorized for the act of preaching.[57]

---

53. Can. 477, § 2; can. 476, § 7.
54. Can. 479, § 1.
55. Can. 483, 1°; Cappello, *Summa*, I, 516-518; De Meester, *Compendium*, II, 359.
56. Can. 529; can. 1338, § 3.
57. Can. 698, § 2.

Hospital chaplains do not have an ecclesiastical office in the strict sense.[58] Hence no obligation of preaching can arise from the office itself. Only in so far as they have been delegated and commanded by the local ordinary, are they obliged to preach on Sundays and feast days of precept. When those who are attached to the hospital find that they are habitually detained from attending the parish Masses, it is meet and just that the hospital chaplain be commanded to preach, in order that such of the hospital's personnel may be able to hear the word of God. Particular law often incorporates such a command for hospital chaplains.

The military chaplain's duties and obligations depend on the specific prescriptions of the Holy See. The faculties which were granted by the Sacred Consistorial Congregation to the Military Ordinariate of the United States on July 1, 1940, authorized the latter to share with chaplains the right "to exercise the care of souls (observing, however, all things required by law) from the time of their appointment to the office of chaplain, with full parochial power."[60] Accordingly the military chaplain had the same duties and obligations as the pastor in relation to the care of souls of the military group to which he was attached. Hence the military chaplain had the obligation to preach on Sundays and on the feast days of precept.

58. Drumm, *Hospital Chaplains,* The Catholic University of America Canon Law Studies, n. 178 (Washington, D. C.: The Catholic University of America Press, 1943), pp. 61-65.

59. Drumm, *Hospital Chaplains,* p. 146.

60. Bouscaren, *The Canon Law Digest,* II, 589.

CHAPTER VI

THE SUBJECT MATTER OF THE OBLIGATION OF PREACHING

ARTICLE I. *The Homily*

Not only does the common law place on those who have the care of souls a grave obligation of preaching, but it also determines, at least in a generic sense, the qualitative subject matter of this obligation. Canon 1344, § 1, obliges the pastor to announce the word of God to the people through the means of the homily.

The homily, taken strictly, is a familiar explanation of the Scriptures ending with moral exhortations.[1] However, here the term is used generally, so that any form of development is adaptable for the Sunday sermon, provided it carries a supernatural message in language which the people can understand.[2] The homily customarily is taken from the gospel of the day, but it may be taken from any part of the gospels. In fact, this is sometimes advisable in order to obtain variety in sermon preaching.[3]

Coronata states that the matter to be treated in the homily is not determined or defined by the law.[4] True, the particular religious topics are not indicated in the law. But since the law does require the delivery of a homily, then, if one accepts that term in the strict sense, the law implicitly requires the treatment of those truths which are contained in the gospel that is to be preached. The reasons why authors hold that the homily should in its concept be understood in a general sense is precisely that the Scriptures are the chief source of the Catholic teaching. So, any treatment of a religious theme, if accommodated to the intelligence of the hearers, seems to suffice for the fulfilling of the law.[5]

Moreover, canon 1347, § 1, states that the subject matter of sermons should be especially the things which the faithful must believe and do

1. Claeys-Bouuaert-Simenon, *Manuale Juris Canonici* (3 vols., Vols. I et III, 3. ed., 1930; Vol. II, 1931, Gandae et Leodii: H. Dessain), III, 113; Fanfani, *De Iure Parochorum*, p. 193.

2. Bouscaren-Ellis, *Canon Law*, p. 687; Mörsdorf, *Die Rechtssprache*, p. 250.

3. Regatillo, *Institutiones*, II, 92.

4. Coronata, *Institutiones*, II, 271.

5. Ayrinhac, *Administrative Legislation of the New Code of Canon Law* (London, New York, Toronto: Longmans, Green & Co., 1930), p. 228 (hereafter cited *Administrative Legislation*).

in order to be saved. It does not seem that this canon refers exclusively to canon 1345; for in canon 1345 the legislator expresses a wish that sermons be preached in churches and public oratories at every Mass on all feast days of precept, leaving to the ordinary discretionary power to prescribe such a practice. Canon 1346, § 1, urges ordinaries to see that sermons are preached more frequently during Lent and Advent; so canon 1347, § 1, does not appear to refer exclusively to canon 1345. It will be noted, rather, that canon 1347, § 1, speaks of sermons in general. Certainly, when the canon refers to sermons in general it also includes reference to the homily, which is a particular form of sermon.

Even though the topical matter of the homily is not specifically determined by the common law, any pastor will find abundant themes for the homily in consequence of an intelligent perusal of the Scriptures, as aided by helpful commentaries, by meditation, and by consultation of the many authors who have written on the subject.

The length of the homily is not determined by the common law. However, particular circumstances of the occasion may well determine its length. Moreover, particular law may require the homily to be of fifteen, ten, or five minutes' duration. Wherever no particular law or instruction exists, the pastor will prudently adjudge the matter according to the spiritual need of his flock.

ARTICLE 2. *The Catechetical Instructions*

Besides stressing the obligation of delivering a homily on Sundays and on feast days of precept, the Council of Trent also commanded that catechetical instructions be given to the faithful on these days.[6] The same law is expressed in canon 1332, which obliges the pastor to give catechetical instructions to the adult faithful.[7]

Can then the obligation of delivering the homily and of giving catechetical instructions be fulfilled at the same time or by means of the same act? Certainly the obligations themselves are distnct, as appears from the Council of Trent,[8] from the regulations of Pope Pius X,[9]

6. Conc. Trident., sess. XXIV, *de ref.*, c. 4, c. 7.

7. Can. 1332.—Diebus dominicis aliisque festis de praecepto, ea hora quae suo iudicio magis apta sit ad populi frequentiam, debet insuper parochus catechismum fidelibus adultis, sermone ad eorum captum accomodato, explicare.

8. Conc. Trident., sess. V, *de ref.*, c. 2; sess. XXIV, *de ref.*, c. 4, c. 7.

9. *Acerbo nimis*, 15 apr. 1905, n. 16, ad VI—*Fontes*, n. 666.

from the Code itself,[10] and from a recent decree of the Sacred Congregation of the Council.[11] That both obligations might be satisfied by means of the same act, it would be necessary that the homily be framed in such a manner so as to include the catechetical instructions. Is this possible?

Ayrinhac (1867-1930), while admitting that the obligations are distinct, nevertheless stated that the two may possibly be combined.[12] It is not clear whether the author means that both obligations may be satisfied by means of one discourse, that is, that the homily be developed in the form of a catechetical instruction, or whether he intends to point structurally to two distinct discourses which are delivered immediately in succession.

Jansen admits the latter manner as a practical way of fulfilling both obligations.[13] Wagner,[14] on the other hand, follows the alternative interpretation, for he admits that the obligations are duly fulfilled by means of one discourse which includes the necessary elements of both the homily and the catechetical instruction.

Augustine (1872-1943) and Woywod (1880-1941) seemed to imply that both obligations may be fulfilled by means of one discourse. Woywod wrote that canon 1332 is based on the European system of divine services, where the catechetical instruction is separated from the Mass and given at some other time of the day, usually in the afternoon. It is the custom in the United States, so wrote this author, that all sermons are delivered during the Mass except on extraordinary occasions such as novenas, retreats, Forty Hours, and the like. He cautioned that the time available for the sermon should not be consumed by multiplied announcements.[15]

Augustine complained that through the law as contained in canons 1332 and 1344 too great a burden is placed on pastors in missionary countries (among which he considered the United States); consequently there should be invoked some kind of modified adaptation in these laws, according to the discretion of the ordinary.[16]

10. Cans. 1332, 1344, 2382.
11. S.C.C., decr. 12 ian. 1935—*AAS*, XXVII (1935), 145-152.
12. *Administrative Legislation*, p. 223.
13. *Canonical Provisions for Catechetical Instruction*, p. 101.
14. *Parochial Substitute Vicars and Supplying Priests*, p. 93, footnote 67.
15. *A Practical Commentary*, II, 99, 104.
16. *A Commentary*, VI, 345.

Coronata holds that the obligations of delivering a homily and of catechetically instructing the adult faithful are two distinct obligations which cannot be fulfilled by means of one and the same discourse.[17] This seemed to be the mind of Pope Pius X when he wrote in his Encyclical Letter *Acerbo nimis* that there are those who believe and judge that they can supplant the catechetical instruction with the homily, but that they are in error. The homily and the catechetical instruction are two different things. The homily presupposes that one already knows the truths of the faith. The catechetical instruction lays the foundation, gives the fundamentals, instructs in the truths of the faith.[18] Even though Pope Pius X spoke and argued here for the necessity of catechetical instructions in general, his words nevertheless are applicable to the point at issue.

How can the pastor fulfill two distinct obligations, and yet for achieving their fulfillment take advantage at the same time of the obligatory presence of the faithful at Mass? The answer depends on the circumstances of the parish. If the parish has two or more scheduled Masses on Sundays and on feast days of precept, the solution seems easy. At the one Mass the pastor will give the homily, and at the other Mass, the catechetical instruction. This would satisfy the obligation as enacted in canon 1332, since the time for giving the catechetical instructions is left to the judgment of the pastor. By alternating the homily and the catechetical instruction at the Masses, the pastor will be able to instruct the great majority of his flock.[19]

If there is only one scheduled Mass in the parish, then the pastor will have to follow the particular legislation. Such would also be the case when a pastor has one Mass in a parish church and another Mass in a distant mission chapel. If pertinent particular legislation is lacking, the pastor will use his own prudent judgment. If in his judgment he decides that the people stand more in need of catechetical instructions, then it seems that there is no prohibition against having the catechetical instruction during the Mass and postponing the homily until Vespers or evening services.[20] If, on the other hand, the pastor judges that his flock is more in need of encouragement and exhortation, then it seems pre-

17. *Institutiones,* II, 271.
18. Litt. encycl., *Acerbo nimis,* 15 apr. 1905, ad XXII—*Fontes,* n. 666.
19. McVann, *The Canon Law on Sermon Preaching,* p. 113.
20. Coronata, *Institutiones,* II, 271.

ferable to have the homily during the Mass and the catechetical instruction at a later time. In rural areas where there is difficulty of convening the faithful for a later service, or when conditions do not warrant a later service, the catechetical instruction could be held before or after the Mass, and the homily during the Mass.

If at some particular time the pastor cannot decide whether the homily or the catechetical instruction should be preferred, he should resolve the doubt by giving preference to the catechetical instruction, since it deals with things which are relatively important and necessary for salvation.[21] In an impasse which makes it necessary for the pastor to forego habitually either the homily or the catechetical instruction, the ordinary should be consulted for a dispensation. The pastor cannot dispense himself.

Cappello, however, maintains that the ordinary cannot allow the omission of the catechetical instructions even on the more solemn feast days, as he can allow the omission of the homily, since the Code is silent about the possible granting of this permission.[22]

Since the ordinary has the primary obligation to see that the word of God is preached and that the faithful are instructed, he certainly can determine the manner in which these duties are to be fulfilled.[23] Some authors, however, declare that the ordinary can, for a just cause, dispense from the obligation of giving the catechetical instructions just as he can dispense from the obligation of delivering the homily.[24]

It must be noted that the obligation of catechetically instructing the adult faithful is a personal obigation of the pastor.[25] When the pastor is not able personally to fulfill this obligation, he must acquire the service of another.[26] Here, as in canon 1344, the assistant cannot habitually fulfill the pastor's obligation unless he has the permission from the ordinary, or unless particular law or regulations have determined the manner in which this obligation should be fulfilled.[27]

---

21. Cappello, *Summa*, I, 487; McVann, *The Canon Law on Sermon Preaching*, p. 114.
22. Cappello, *Summa*, I, 489.
23. Cans. 335, 1327.
24. Cocchi, *Commentarium*, VI, 44; Regatillo, *Institutiones*, II, 89; Berutti, *Institutiones*, IV, 345.
25. Coronata, *Institutiones*, II, 256; Wernz-Vidal, *Ius Canonicum*, IV, pars II, 51.
26. Vermeersch-Creusen, *Epitome*, II, n. 666.
27. Jansen, *Canonical Provisions for Catechetical Instructions*, pp. 82-83.

ARTICLE 3.

Canon 1345 and the III Plenary Council of Baltimore (1884)

Realizing the importance of sermon preaching, the legislator introduced a substantially new element in canon 1345. This canon expresses the ardent wish that at every Mass which the faithful attend in all churches and public oratories on holy days of obligation there be a short explanation of the gospel or of some part of Christian doctrine. The first part of this canon expresses only a directive. The second part, however, gives the ordinary the right to make preceptive regulations in this regard. If the ordinary has commanded that a short sermon on the gospel of the day or on some part of Christian doctrine be held at every Mass on holy days of obligation, then not only the secular clergy but also the religious and the regular clergy are bound by this regulation. The obligation is binding on all who have the care of souls, whether in a parish church or in a public oratory.

The Fathers of the III Plenary Council of Baltimore (1884) made such a preceptive regulation when they commanded that on every Sunday and feast day of precept, even in the summertime, at all Masses whether private, or sung, or solemn, or early in the morning, the gospel of the day be read in the vernacular and a five-minute sermon be preached, every custom and pretext to the contrary notwithstanding.[28] This law as expressed in the III Plenary Council of Baltimore is apposite to canon 1345. True, it demands a sermon not only at every Mass on the holy days as does canon 1345, but it also demands a sermon at all the Masses on Sundays. This law does not militate against the law of the Code. Therefore the law of the III Plenary Council of Baltimore is still in effect.[29] Accordingly it binds throughout the United States. The local ordinary can dispense from this law only in particular cases and then only for a just cause.[30] Consequently those who have the care of souls and fail to preach at all Masses on Sundays and holy days of obligation are, if not sinning against the common law, at least sinning against the law of the III Plenary Council of Baltimore.

---

28. *Acta et Decreta Conc. Balt. III*, n. 216.
29. Can. 6, 1°.
30. Can. 291, § 2.

What, for instance, is to be said about the practice of not preaching at an early Mass throughout the entire year? The III Plenary Council of Baltimore expressly demanded a sermon even at a very early Mass. Ordinarily there could be found sufficient time for a sermon at least of five minutes' duration. There can exist circumstances in which a Mass must be celebrated shortly after midnight for a particular group of workers. An example is the Mass which serves the convenience of the printers of a newspaper. If a sermon were never preached to such a group at the Mass which they attend, it seems to the writer that the salvation of their souls could become gravely endangered. Certainly a well prepared five-minute sermon can do much good. To demand the giving of such a sermon does not seem to the writer to cause great inconvenience to the priest or to the faithful. The writer, however, would admonish the priest who is placed in such circumstances to seek the advice of the ordinary. His judgment in the matter will be the norm of action. After all, the ordinary can dispense in such a case.[31]

---

31. Can. 2[illegible], § 2.

Chapter VII

THE TIME AND PLACE FOR FULFILLING THE OBLIGATION OF PREACHING

ARTICLE 1. *The Time*

The law of the Church has designated the particular days on which a sermon must be preached. Canon 1344, § 1, requires the pastor to preach the homily during the Mass at which the greater number of the parishioners attends every Sunday and holy day of obligation throughout the year.

According to canon 1247, § 1, besides the Sundays of the year, the holy days of obligation for the universal Church are ten in number. They are the feasts of the Nativity of Our Lord (December 25); of the Circumcision of Our Lord (January 1); of the Epiphany (January 6); of the Ascension; of Corpus Christi; of the Immaculate Conception (December 8); of the Assumption of the Blessed Virgin Mary (August 15); of St. Joseph (March 19); of Saints Peter and Paul (June 29); and of All Saints (November 1).

However these holy days are not all observed in the United States. In the III Plenary Council of Baltimore the Papal Legate, His Eminence, James Cardinal Gibbons, petitioned Rome on December 23, 1884, for an abrogation and a transfer of some of these holy days of obligation. The reply granting the request was dated November 25, 1885.[1] In the decrees of this council six days were determined for observance as holy days of obligation in the United States. These six days were the feasts of the Nativity of Our Lord (December 25); of the Circumcision of Our Lord (January 1); of the Ascension; of the Immaculate Conception (December 8); of the Assumption of the Blessed Virgin Mary (August 15); and of All Saints (November 1).[2] These six days alone need to be observed as holy days of obligation in the United States even today, since the third paragraph of canon 1247 expressly states that, if any of the ten named holy days of obligation have been anywhere abolished or transferred, nothing shall be changed without the advice of the Apostolic See.[3]

---

1. *Acta et Decreta Conc. Balt. III*, pp. CV-CVIII.
2. *Acta et Decreta Conc. Balt. III*, n. 111
3. Can. 1247, § 3.—Sicubi aliquod festum ex enumeratis legitime sit abolitum vel translatum, nihil inconsulta Sede Apostolica innovetur.

Consequently, in the United States the pastor must preach the homily on every Sunday of the year and on the six enumerated holy days of obligation. The delivery of the homily is not required on the other four suppressed or transferred holy days of obligation, at least not in the United States. If the holy day has been transferred to the following Sunday, then the two obligations as deriving from the Sunday and the transferred holy day can be fulfilled by means of the delivery of a single homily.[4]

Moreover, the legislator desires that the word of God be preached during the Mass.[5] It has been the practice in the Church for many centuries to preach during the Mass. This practice is still maintained, and the directive for it is contained in the Roman Missal.[6]

There seems, however, to be no strict obligation to preach the homily during the Mass. Canon 1344, § 1, does not enact such an obligation, since it uses the words, *especially during the Mass.* And the words used in the Roman Missal seem to be directive rather than preceptive. Certainly the homily does not belong to the essential rubrics of the Mass. It is rather to be considered as a lawful interruption of the Mass. Consequently, there is no strict obligation to deliver the homily during the Mass. It is, though, altogether proper that the homily be delivered immediately after the gospel of the Mass, since ordinarily it is an explanation of the gospel to which are added words of encouragement and exhortation. For any just cause the homily can be delivered before or after the Mass, or at some other time of the day.[7]

The homily should be delivered during that Mass at which the greater attendance of the faithful is in evidence.[8] This is rather a logical conclusion; for in having the care of souls the pastor is in duty bound to teach and preach to the faithful of his parish. The pastor can fulfill this obligation in no better manner than by taking advantage of the obligatory attendance of the greater number of his parishioners at Mass.

---

4. Blat, *Commentarium,* Lib. III, partes II-IV, 270.

5. Can. 1344, § 1: . . . . . . praesertim intra Missam in qua maior soleat esse populi frequentia. . . . . . .

6. *Ritus servandus in celebratione Missae,* VI, n. 6: Si autem sit praedicandum, concionator, finito Evangelio, praedicet, et sermone sive contione expleta, dicatur Credo, vel si non sit dicendum, cantetur Offertorium.

7. Coronata, *Institutiones,* II, 271.

8. Can. 1344, § 1.

On the other hand, if particular law has commanded that a short explanation of the gospel or of some point of Christian doctrine be given at every Mass on Sundays and holy days of obligation, everyone, whether of the secular clergy or of the religious and regular clergy, is bound by this law as long as he is within the territorial jurisdiction wherein the particular law has force. Since the III Plenary Council of Baltimore has promulgated such a law which is still operative, a short sermon must be held at all Masses on every Sunday and holy day of obligation. The law of the council expressly prescribed the sermon during the celebration of Mass. Consequently this law would not be fulfilled if the sermon were not held during the Mass. There is no option for the preaching of the sermon at some other hour of the day outside of Mass.[9]

In addition to the above mentioned times at which the pastor is obliged to preach, the legislator has placed an obligation on local ordinaries to see that sermons are preached in cathedral and parochial churches with greater frequency during Lent. The obligation placed on the ordinary demands that he insist on the preaching of sermons on other days during the Lenten season besides the Sundays and the holy days of obligation.[10]

The Council of Trent formerly demanded a sermon every day, or at least three times a week, during Lent.[11] The law of the Code, however, is not that strict. It leaves the particular details, that is, the indication of the frequency, the arrangement of the hours and the designation of the topics to the judgment of the ordinary.[12]

The law of the Code also obliges the local ordinaries to see that in cathedral and parochial churches sermons are preached more frequently during Advent, if they deem it expedient.[13] Here the obligation is conditional, depending on the local ordinary's judgment of the prudence and the expediency of holding such sermons.

It is the custom in the United States, particularly where no specific regulations are given, to hold services on Wednesday and Friday nights during Lent. A well developed sermon is preached on Wednesday nights.

9. Can. 291, § 2.
10. Cocchi, *Commentarium*, VI, 59.
11. Sess. XXIV, *de ref.*, c. 4.
12. Can. 1346, § 1; Augustine, *A Commentary*, VI, 367.
13. Can. 1346, § 1.

The Friday night services usually consist of the Way of the Cross. There seems not to be anything like a general practice of holding particular services during Advent.[14] The local ordinary is not negligent in his duty in this regard if he allows such a practice to continue in his diocese.

It is noteworthy that the decrees and the interpretations of the Sacred Congregations regarding sermons preached at night no longer seem to be in effect. They became abrogated through contrary custom and in consequence of the changing habits of the people even long before the advent of the present Code. Moreover, the Code is completely silent concerning the giving of sermons at a nocturnal hour.[15] Hence even on that score alone, in line with the principle which according to canon 6, 6°, rules out the continued application of a disciplinary law which no longer receives any kind of mention in the Code, the past legislation in this matter must be regarded as having lost all binding force.

When such sermons are held during Lent and Advent (if the latter practice obtains), the pastor cannot omit the homily and the catechetical instruction on Sundays and on holy days of obligation. Any contrary custom cannot be sustained.[16]

The law does not require the pastor to preach the Lenten sermons. He may, therefore, obtain the service of some other priest who is approved for preaching.[17]

In cathedral and parochial churches which have chapters, the canons and the others who belong to the chapter, unless they are lawfully impeded, must attend the Lenten or Advent sermons if these are held immediately after the choir service. The ordinary can compel them to attend.[18]

Even though the Code does not speak of the need of Lenten or Advent sermons in collegiate churches, yet Vermeersch-Creusen and Augustine require that in the event such sermons are held the canons be present for the sermons, for their attendance seems to be part of their obligation as members of the choir.[19] This opinion is confirmed by two

---

14. Woywod, *A Practical Commentary*, II, 105.
15. Wernz-Vidal, *Ius Canonicum*, IV, pars II, 44.
16. Cans. 1332, 1344, 2382; cf. Coranata, *Institutiones*, II, 271; Cocchi, *Commentarium*, VI, 59; Augustine, *A Commentary*, VI, 365.
17. Bouscaren-Ellis, *Canon Law*, p. 688.
18. Can. 1346, § 2.
19. Vermeersch-Creusen, *Epitome, II*, n. 680; Augustine, *A Commentary*, VI, 367.

decrees of the Sacred Congregation of Rites.[20] However in the United States where chapters do not exist, the priests attached to the cathedral or parochial churches are not bound to attend the Lenten and Advent sermons.

The local ordinary may command that sermons be held on particular days and at particular hours.[21] The local ordinary also can forbid sermon preaching at certain times and hours. The law of the Code allows the episcopal ordinary to forbid preaching at the time when he himself preaches, or when he has others to preach before him for a public and extraordinary cause, unless on such occassions the preaching is done in large cities.[22]

The episcopal ordinary cannot forbid preaching in the large cities during the time of his own sermon or of the sermon which someone else preaches in his presence at some public and extraordinary gathering of the faithful. A city is consideed as large when it has one hundred thousand inhabitants, even if the majority of that number are non-Catholics.[23]

Pruemmer and Augustine felt that the episcopal ordinary, even when he preaches in his own person, can forbid preaching in the other local churches only when he gives the sermon for a public and extraordinary cause.[24] But the clause, "*ex causa publica atque extraordinaria,*" refers specifically and exclusively to the case when the bishop has called on someone else to preach in his presence.[25] In the above mentioned cases the episcopal ordinary can forbid sermons even in parochial churches, if the city is not large. This is altogether proper, since the chief shepherd of souls as a successor of the Apostles is preaching.[26] But in large cities the episcopal ordinary cannot forbid the preaching of sermons in parochial churches at the time during which he preaches or has others to preach in his presence for a public and extraordinary cause.[27]

---

20. S.R.C., *Callien.*, 22 mart. 1653—*Decreta Authentica Congregationis Sacorum Rituum* (6 vols., Romae: Ex Typographia Polyglotta, 1898-1927), n. 944 (hereafter abbreviated *DA*); S.R.C., *Placentina*, 10 dec. 1718, ad IV—*DA*, n. 2258.

21. Wernz-Vidal, *Ius Canonicum*, IV, pars II, 45.

22. Can. 1343, § 2.

23. Cocchi, *Commentarium*, VI, 57; Vermeersch-Creusen, *Epitome*, II, n. 678; Coronata, *Institutiones*, II, 269.

24. Pruemmer, *Manuale Iuris Canonici*, q. 405, 5, p. 486; Augustine, *A Commentary*, VI, 363.

25. Beste, *Introductio in Codicem*, p. 671; Vermeersch-Creusen, *Epitome*, II, n. 678.

26. Vermeersch-Creusen, *loc. cit.*

27. Coronata, *loc. cit.*; Vermeersch-Creusen, *loc. cit.*

The local ordinary, however, cannot forbid exempt religious to preach at the same hour at which pastors preach in the parochial churches. This right is not granted by the law of the Code.[28]

ARTICLE 2. *The Place*

In the early history of the Church the sermon was preached in divers places. However, for many centuries past the church building has been considered as the proper place for the preaching of sermons. In every church today one usually finds a pulpit, or an elevated dais, from which the word of God is made known to the faithful. The law of the Code, however, does not demand a pulpit in the church edifice.

Canon 1344, which places on pastors the obligation of preaching, does not explicitly state that the sermon should be held in the parish church. But implicitly, by pointing to the pastor's duty to preach the sermon especially during the Mass, the law involves the consequence that the sermon should be delivered in the parish church. Moreover, the continued practice of the preaching of sermons in the church seems to make the obligation of the pastor a local one, that is, the pastor then fulfills the obligation of canon 1344 when he preaches in the parish church.[29]

The pastor has the care of souls of a particular parish. The law demands that every parish have its own church wherein the sacred ministry is exercised.[30]

There arises, then, the question whether the pastor is obliged to preach in filial churches and confraternity churches or in oratories which exist within his parish limits. The writer is of the opinion that by the law of canon 1344 the pastor is not bound to preach in these churches or oratories. The pastor fully satisfies this law when he preaches in his own parish church. Of course, the pastor could preach in these churches or oratories without any special permission as long as the ordinary has not exempted these churches or oratories from his jurisdiction.[31] Moreover, if it is necessary to use the filial or confraternity churches or oratories in order to accommodate the faithful of the parish, it would be the

28. Wernz-Vidal, *Ius Canonicum*, IV, pars II, 45.
29. Hinschius, *Das Kirchenrecht*, IV, 373-374.
30. Cans. 216, § 1; 1154; 1161.
31. Can. 464.

pastor's obligation to see that sermons are preached in them, although he himself would not be bound to preach in them if he preached in the parish church.[32] In such instances the pastor could nominate the preachers, but it is the local ordinary who is authorized in the law to grant them the faculty for preaching.[33]

In semi-public oratories the local ordinary can command that sermons be preached at every Mass. Yet he may also forbid the preaching of sermons in the semi-public oratory, especially if it may do an injustice to the parish church. Since the semi-public oratory is not erected for the good of the faithful in general, the local ordinary can make such regulations.[34]

In non-parochial churches and public oratories the ordinary can command that a sermon be preached at every Mass celebrated therein on Sundays and holy days of obligation.[35] However, it does not appear that the local ordinary can entirely prohibit sermon preaching in non-parochial churches or in public oratories. It appears also that the local ordinary cannot forbid the attendance of the faithful at the Masses at which no sermon is preached in these churches or oratories. The faithful, at least some, would have a right to attend Mass in the public oratory or the non-parochial church, and the ordinary cannot take away this right altogether.[36]

The ordinary can forbid sermons to be preached outside of a church or an oratory, as, for example, at an outdoor public gathering, or over the radio. The diocesan faculties must be consulted regarding such possible regulations. If the diocesan faculties restrict the preaching of sermons in this manner, then all the priests of the diocese are bound by this restriction, whether they be seculars or religious. Even pastors, though in virtue of their office they enjoy the right of preaching, are bound by whatever diocesan regulations of this kind that may exist.

---

32. Fanfani, *De Iure Parochorum*, p. 192.
33. Cans. 1337; 1341, § 2.
34. Feldhaus, *Oratories*, The Catholic University of America Canon Law Studies, n. 42 (Washington, D. C.: The Catholic University of America, 1927), p. 100; Berutti, *Institutiones*, IV, 358.
35. Cans. 1171; 483.
36. Feldhaus, *Oratories*, pp. 101-102.

CHAPTER VIII

CONCILIAR AND SYNODAL LAW CONCERNING PREACHING

ARTICLE 1. *The Scope of Particular Law*

The Code of Canon Law as the legislation of the Catholic Church has binding force on all who by baptism have been initiated into the membership of this Church unless they have been expressly exempted. Since this legislation is universal, it naturally abstracts from consideration of particular local circumstances. Even though the laws as expressed in the Code of Canon Law have universal binding force, yet often there are occasions and circumstances in which the general laws must be particularized if they are to reach and have their full juridical effect. The universal Church therefore in its hierarchical and monarchical constitution presents the way for the specification and particularization of its general laws.

The bishops, who are the successors of the Apostles, have complete legislative power in their dioceses. This episcopal legislative power, however, is limited in so far that it cannot enact laws that are contrary to the divine, the natural, or the general ecclesiastical law. In the particularization of the general ecclesiastical law episcopal enactments usually go beyond the general ecclesiastical law, that is, they require more than the general laws require.

The particularization of the general laws may be accomplished in three diverse manners, namely, through the legislation of a plenary council, through the enactments of a provincial council, and through the statutes of a diocesan synod.

The plenary council is one at which all the bishops of a nation or a people, or also the bishops of a number of ecclesiastical provinces, meet under the recognition of the Roman Pontiff, whose legate presides.[1] The laws enacted in such a plenary council, after being reviewed and recognized by the Supreme Pontiff through the Sacred Congregation of the Council, have binding force for the universal territory of such a nation or people, or of the various provinces which shared in the conciliar action. The local ordinary can dispense from these particular laws of the plenary council only in individual cases and for a just cause.[2]

---

1. Can. 281.
2. Can. 291.

The provincial council is the meeting of all the bishops of an ecclesiastical province. According to the present discipline the provincial council is to be held at least every twenty years.[3] The metropolitan is to convene and preside at the provincial council, and needs no special permission from the Supreme Pontiff to do so. If the metropolitan is legitimately impeded or if the metropolitan see is vacant, the suffragan bishop who is the elder in promotion to the suffragan sees has the right to convene and preside at the provincial council.[4] The laws enacted in the provincial council, after they have been reviewed and recognized by the Sacred Congregation of the Council, have binding force for the entire province. Likewise, the local ordinary can dispense from the particular laws of the provincial council only in individual cases and for a just cause.[5]

The diocesan synod is a legitimate meeting of the clergy who in some manner belong to the diocese and who have been convened by the bishop to treat of those things which are necessary and useful for the spiritual welfare of the clergy and the faithful of a particular diocese. The diocesan synod is according to the present discipline to be held at least every ten years.[6] The bishop, however, is the sole legislator in the diocesan synod. All others present at the synod have only a consultative vote.[7] The statutes emanating from the synod have the binding force of law, since they proceed from true episcopal legislative power. The bishop can dispense from synodal laws for any reason he deems sufficient.[8]

According to the general norm of canon 13, § 2, particular laws are binding only on the subjects of a territory, that is, on those who have a domicile or a quasi-domicile and also actually reside within the territory. One may however raise the question whether strangers (*peregrini*) are bound by these particular laws. The stranger is not bound by the particular laws of his own territory when he is outside his territory, unless such particular laws are personal laws, or unless their violation outside the territory occasions harm also within the territory. Pastors and those who have the care of souls are nevertheless bound, even when absent

3. Can. 283.
4. Can. 284.
5. Can. 291.
6. Cans. 356, § 1; 358.
7. Can. 362.
8. Can. 82.

from their territory, by the particular laws of their territory in matters concerning preaching, for the transgression of such particular laws brings harm to their own territory.[9] Strangers are not bound by the particular laws of the territory in which they are present, except by the particular laws which concern the public order or which prescribe certain legal formalities.[10] The particular laws on preaching are not binding on the stranger who comes into the territory, since he lacks the subjection which constitutes the very touchstone of the law's possible application to him.

ARTICLE 2. *Scope of Particular Law Concerning Preaching*

a. The Canonical Mission

While the general law determines that the local ordinary alone grants both to the secular and to the non-exempt religious clergy the faculty for preaching, particular law may determine the manner in which the faculty is to be given, especially to extradiocesan priests. The IV Provincial Council of Portland in Oregon (1932) declared that no extradiocesan priest should be invited to preach unless first the permission of the ordinary has been obtained. This permission should be obtained in writing as a rule.[11]

The IV Synod of Green Bay (1920) clearly declared that no one is allowed to exercise the office of preaching in the diocese unless he has received either a parochial benefice, or the office of preaching, or the faculty for preaching as granted by the local ordinary.[12]

The I Synod of Toledo in Ohio (1941) stated that the preaching faculties for the visiting clergy must be obtained from the local ordinary except as provided for in the episcopal document, n. 30. There it is stated that the pastors may delegate the authorization for preaching within their own territory to any priest in good standing.[13]

---

9. Can. 14, § 1, 1°.

10. Can. 14, § 1, 2°.

11. *Acta et Decreta Concilii Provincialis Portlandensis in Oregon Quarti, diebus VIII, IX, X Septembris 1932 habiti* (Portland, Oregon: The Sentinel Printery, 1934) decretum 17 (hereafter cited *IV Conc. Prov. Portlandensis*).

12. *Constitutiones Dioeceseos Sinus Viridis quae in Synodo Dioecesana Quarta, diebus 14-15-16 Decembris 1920 habita, latae et promulgatae fuerunt* (Pulaski, Wisc.: Typis Franciscanae Typographiae, 1921), n. 282 (hereafter cited *IV Syn. Dioec. Sinus Viridis*).

13. *Acta et Decreta Synodi Dioecesanae Toletanae Primae, a 1941* (Toleti: Cancellaria Curiae Dioecesanae, 1941), n. 281 (hereafter cited *I Syn. Dioec. Toletanae*).

The I Synod of Fargo (1941) also determined that extradiocesan priests are not to be invited to preach unless first the permission of the local ordinary has been obtained, or unless the approval of the rural dean has been granted.[14]

b. The Time

The obligation of preaching as incumbent on those who have the care of souls has definitely been established by the general law of the Church. Hence the particular law does not determine anything about the obligation itself; it simply presupposes this grave obligation as existing. The particular law determines rather the time for the fulfilling of the obligation. It specifies the days on which one must preach, and it indicates the length of the sermon or the instruction that one is to give.

As indicated in the third chapter of this work, the provincial councils and diocesan synods which were held after the Council of Trent usually restated the law of this ecumenical council and then determined the length of the sermon. The diocesan synods which were held in the United States before the promulgation of the Code usually quoted the law on preaching as enacted in the III Plenary Council of Baltimore.

Since the promulgation of the Code, the IV Provincial Council of Portland in Oregon decreed that in every church in all the Masses celebrated for the convenience of the faithful on all the Sundays and also, whenever time permitted, on all the holy days of obligation the gospel of the day be read and thereafter explained. The explanation however should be short, not exceeding twenty minutes.[15]

Since this is the only provincial council that has been held in the United States after the promulgation of the Code, all other particular legislation as here considered emanated from the diocesan synods.

The IV Synod of Green Bay (1920) and the Synod of Des Moines (1923) prescribed that on all Sundays and holy days of obligation throughout the year a five-minute instruction be given at all low Masses and a properly so-called sermon, not over half an hour in length, be delivered at the sung, or parochial, or late Mass.[16]

---

14. *Synodus Dioecesana Fargensis Prima, diebus XXIX et XXX Septembris, A.D. 1941 habita* (Milwauchiae: Ex Typographia Bruce, 1941), Articulus XXXII, *De Sacris Concionibus,* statutum 530 (hereafter cited *I Syn. Dioec. Fargensis*).

15. *IV Conc. Prov. Portlandensis,* decretum 15, §§ 1-2.

16. *IV Syn. Dioec. Sinus Viridis,* n. 283; *The Code of the Diocese of Des Moines decreed in Diocesan Synod, held June 15, 1923, and promulgated September 8, 1923,* n. 278 (hereafter cited *Dioc. Syn. of Des Moines*).

The XI Synod of Syracuse (1921) required a ten-minute sermon at all Masses on Sundays and holy days of obligation; but at the principal Mass the sermon should be of about a half hour's duration.[17]

The XXVII Synod of Buffalo (1924) prescribed that in all parish churches every Sunday in all the Masses at least a ten-minute sermon be held. In the more frequented parishes, however, in the first Mass, if time did not allow for it, the sermon could be omitted. On holy days at the principal Mass a ten-minute sermon on the feast of the day was to be given. In all the other Masses on holy days it was permitted to omit the sermon if the pastor judged it advisable to do so.[18]

The I Synod of Salt Lake City (1929) demanded that pastors preach the homily (customary sermon) at the principal Mass on all Sundays and holy days of obligation; in all other Masses on these days a five- or ten-minute sermon or instruction was to be held.[19] Although the length of the homily was not specified, it was according to the obvious wording of the statute not required to be longer than ten minutes.

The IX Synod of Philadelphia (1934) required that a set sermon of at least twenty minutes' duration be preached at the late Mass on Sundays except in the summertime. On all Sundays at every Mass, even during the summer months, however, the gospel of the day was to be read in the vernacular and the congregation was to be instructed for at least five minutes despite any custom or pretext to the contrary.[20]

The I Synod of Toledo (1941) stated that no priest shall omit the sermon at the Sunday and holy day Masses, not even during the summer months or vacation periods, unless a particular necessity intervenes. Moreover, this synod declared that at all Sunday Masses the sermon ordinarily shall not be less than fifteen minutes, nor shall it notably exceed this limit.[21]

---

17. *Synodus Dioecesana Syracusensis Undecima, die XVIII Septembris 1921 habita* (Rochester, N. Y.: Typis Joannis P. Smith Printing Co., 1922), Tit. III, n. 12 (hereafter cited *XI Syn. Dioec. Syracusensis*).

18. *Synodus Dioecesana Buffalensis Vigesima Septima, die 14 Maii 1924* (Buffalo: Union and Times Press, 1924), art. 446 (hereafter cited *XXVII Syn. Dioec. Buffalensis*).

19. *Statuta Dioecesis Lacus Salsi lata et promulgata in Synodo Dioecesana Prima, die 17 Junii 1929 habita* (Bronx N. Y.: New York Catholic Protectory, 1929), n. 178 (hereafter cited *I Syn. Dioec. Lacus Salsi*).

20. *Synodus Dioecesana Philadelphiensis IX, habita die vigesima sexta Aprilis, A.D. 1934 in Sacello Sti. Martini, Overbrook,* statutum LII.

21. *I Syn. Dioec. Toletanae,* n. 282, 283.

The I Synod of Fargo (1941) stated that in all Masses on Sundays and holy days of obligation there should be delivered a sermon adapted to the understanding and the spiritual needs of the faithful. This sermon should not exceed twenty minutes.[22]

c. The Subject Matter

While canon 1344 commands that a homily be delivered every Sunday and holy day of obligation, it is evident that this is not sufficient for the present day conditions. In almost every parish church more than one Mass is required for the accommodation of the faithful. In view of this fact particular legislation not only imposes the obligation of preaching at all the Masses on Sundays and holy days of obligation, but also determines the subject matter of the sermons to be preached at the Masses. Moreover, the wish as expressed in canon 1345, that short instructions be held at every Mass celebrated on Sundays and holy days, has become a reality in view of the obligation as enacted by particular law.

The IV Provincial Council of Portland in Oregon left an option regarding the subject matter of the Sunday and holy day sermon. There was to be either an explanation of the gospel, or an expounding of some part of Christian doctrine. However, the council urged the local ordinaries to institute an outline of sermons and catechetical instructions.[23]

In most of the synodal laws of the United States which were examined by the writer a distinction seemed to be made between the sermon (*concio*) and the short instructions. In most of the cases it was not determined what exactly was to be understood by the terms sermon and instruction. However, according to the ordinary interpretation, an instruction is the exposition or explanation of a point of Christian doctrine. On the other hand, the sermon is understood as a homiletic discourse of some length which expounds a certain truth of religion. Thus a number of synods, without further determining the subject matter, simply com-

22. *I Syn. Dioec. Fargensis,* art. XXXII, *De Sacris Concionibus,* statutum 518 et statutum 519.

23. *IV Prov. Conc. Portlandensis,* statutum 15, §§ 1-2.

manded that a sermon be held at one of the Masses, and a short instruction at the other Masses.[24]

However, several synods did specify the subject matter of preaching. The I Synod of Monterey-Fresno (1929) commanded that the homily, that is, the explanation of the gospel, be held at the parochial Mass, but that in all the other Masses there should be a catechetical sermon or instruction, which was to follow the program of catechetical instructions as assigned for the day in accord with the annual outline furnished by the bishop.[25]

The I Synod of Toledo did not specify the kind of sermon to be delivered on Sundays and holy days of obligation, but it commanded the pastors and the assistants to follow the diocesan sermon plan at least in substance.[26]

In other statutes this synod prescribed the particular subject matter to be treated in sermons throughout the year. It urged, for instance, that papal encyclical letters and pastoral letters of the ordinary be made known and explained to the people in sermons on Sundays. It prescribed that sermons on the sacrament of matrimony be held during Lent,[27] and on the office and prerogatives of the Holy Father during the Pentecost season. Moreover, it commanded that one sermon at least every year should be held in every parish on the priestly and religious vocations, preferably during the month of October.[28] This synod allowed the preaching of a sermon at funerals, but forbade all kinds of eulogies. It also forbade the preaching of any sermon at all at the funerals of suicides and public sinners who received the sacraments *in extremis*.[29]

The I Synod of Fargo, on the other hand, commanded that every sermon on Sundays and holy days of obligation be of a catechetical nature.

---

24. *Statuta Dioeceseos Pittsburgensis in Synodo Dioecesana XIV lata, die 8 Octobris 1919* (Pittsburgh, Pa.: St. Joseph's Protectory Print, 1920), n. 205; *IV Syn. Dioec. Sinus Viridis*, nn. 283, 284; *XI Syn. Dioec. Syracusensis*, Tit. III, n. 12; *Statuta Synodi Altunensis Primae, III Kal. Decembris MCMXXII* (Lancaster, Pa.: Wickersham Printing Co., 1923), Cap. XII, n. 87; *Dioc. Syn. of Des Moines*, n. 278; *XXVII Syn. Dioec. Buffalensis*, art. 446; *I Syn. Dioec. Lacus Salsi*, n. 178; *III Syn. Dioec. Richmondiensis*, statutum 175.

25. *Statuta Dioecesis Montereyensis-Fresnensis in Prima Synodo Dioecesana, diebus 29 et 30 Octobris 1929 lata et promulgata* (Fresni: Sumptibus Saint Columba Guild), statutum 83.

26. *I Syn. Dioec. Toletanae*, n. 283.

27. Cf. Can. 1018.

28. *I Syn. Dioec. Toletanae*, nn. 287, 288, 289.

29. *I Syn. Dioec. Toletanae*, nn. 297, 301, 302.

But it allowed the preaching of a homily on the solemn and special feast days. The catechism of the Council of Trent was made the basis for the prescribed catechetical sermons; all the matter was to be treated within a five-year period.[30]

This synod likewise determined the subject matter of sermons to be held throughout the year. During Lent formal sermons on the principal duties of the Christian life were to be preached. It also urged that there be sermons on marriage during Lent and Advent. Twice a year instructions relative to mixed marriage were to be given. Sermons on the priesthood were to be held on the ember days, and on the religious life during the month of May.[31]

In Canada, the II Synod of Quebec (1940) commanded that in all Masses on Sundays and holy days of obligation the homily should be preached. The synod explained that the homily may be a brief exposition of the gospel or of some part of Christian doctrine. Even though on the more solemn feast days a special sermon be held, nevertheless there should also be a short explanation of the gospel of the day.[32]

This same synod commanded that during Lent in the cathedral and in all the parish churches, in addition to the Sunday sermons, sermons on the principal tenets of Christian doctrine, and especially on the necessity and the characteristics of penance, be preached to the people three times or at least twice a week.[33]

ARTICLE 3. *Faculties*

The diocesan faculties may be considered under the general heading of particular law, since they are the powers given by the ordinary to the priests of his own territory. Motry defines a faculty as the power which an ecclesiastical superior, endowed with jurisdiction in the respective forum, grants to a subject for placing or omitting an act beyond or against the law validly or licitly or at least safely.[34]

---

30. *I Syn. Dioec. Fargensis,* Art. XXXII, *De Sacris Concionibus,* statutum 518.

31. *I Syn. Dioec. Fargensis,* Art. XXXII *De Sacris Concionibus,* statutum 519, 2; cf. also statuta 153, 325, 334, 362 of this Synod.

32. *Acta et Decreta Synodi Dioecesanae Quebecensis Secundae, a. 1940* (Quebeci: Cancellaria Curiae Metropolitanae, 1940), decretum 398 (hereafter cited *II Syn. Dioec. Quebecensis*).

33. *II Syn. Dioec. Quebecensis,* decretum 401.

34. Motry, *Diocesan Faculties according to the Code of Canon Law,* The Catholic University of America Canon Law Studies, n. 16 (Washington, D. C.: The Catholic University of America, 1922), p. 17 (hereafter cited *Diocesan Faculties*).

The faculty to preach is granted to pastors at the moment of their installation in the pastoral office, as it is indicated in chapter V of this work. The faculty for preaching which is granted to the other priests of the diocese, however, may be given under certain conditions. For the most part, the faculty for preaching is granted unconditionally to the priests in the majority of the dioceses in the United States. Some of the dioceses, however, make the restriction that the priests may preach only in parish churches, or only in other churches, but not to members of lay religious or non-exempt religious institutes.[35]

Those who have the right to preach by reason of their office, or by delegation, are not allowed to delegate that right or faculty to others.[36]

But the faculties of some dioceses do grant to pastors or to rural deans the right to allow other priests to preach under certain conditions.[37]

It may be mentioned that the faculty for preaching includes the right to give catechetical instructions, unless the ordinary has expressly withheld this right.[38]

---

35. Snee-Clark, *Synthesis of the Diocesan Faculties in the United States* (Woodstock, Md.: Woodstock College Press, 1948), nn. 358-364, pp. 31-32.

36. Cans. 1337 and 1341, § 2.

37. Snee-Clark, *Synthesis of Diocesan Faculties in the United States*, nn. 365-382, pp. 32-33.

38. Motry, *Diocesan Faculties*, p. 143.

Chapter IX

PENAL SANCTIONS

Article 1. *The Penal Removal from Office*

The common law of the Church in canon 2382 by means of a penal sanction fortifies the observance of the pastor's obligation of preaching and of giving catechetical instructions. This canon states:

> Si parochus graviter neglexerit Sacramentorum adminstrationem, infirmorum assistentiam, puerorum populique institutionem, concionem diebus dominicis ceterisque festis, custodiam ecclesiae paroecialis, sanctissimae Eucharistiae, sacrorum oleorum, ab Ordinario coerceatur ad normam can. 2182-2185.

To understand the nature of the penalty contained in canon 2382 it is necessary to invoke an exposition of canons 2182-2185, which treat of the penal administrative procedure against negligent pastors. It is to be noted that the penalty is not of a *latae sententiae*, but of a *ferendae sententiae* character. Moreover, in this procedure the penalties are applied gradually: the admonition, the reprimand and punishment, the deprivation of the fruits of the office or benefice, and finally the removal from office or benefice.

This penal administrative procedure against a pastor who has been negligent in regard to preaching and catechizing begins with the canonical admonition.[1] The infliction of any canonical punishment, however, presupposes a canonical delict, that is, an external and morally imputable violation of law which is fortified at least with an indeterminate canonical sanction.[2] The bishop therefore must have moral certainty of the presence of such a delict. The gravity of the delict must be fully certified. The gravity of negligence has been discussed in article 2 of Chapter V of this work. There it was maintained that the canonical penalties were to be applied to one who has been negligent in preaching for three continuous months. Even though a shorter period of time may be considered by some as constituting grave negligence and a grave sin, nevertheless the period of three continuous months certainly and unquestionably demon-

1. Can. 2182.
2. Can. 2195, § 1.

strates that the negligence on the part of the pastor is delictual, arising out of contumacy or total disregard for the law.

Moreover, the bishop must ascertain the fact of negligence not from rumors, private denunciations or complaints, but rather from the rural deans, the commission of vigilance, and from the priests associated with the supposedly delinquent pastor.[3]

Since the removal from office is an unpleasant affair which should be avoided if at all possible, the bishop should proceed cautiously and prudently in inflicting these penalties. The Code of Canon Law recommends such a manner of acting.[4]

Hence, before applying the law of canon 2182, the bishop may give a paternal admonition to the negligent pastor, so that he may be able to check his carelessness in this matter.[5] This is not the canonical admonition mentioned in canon 2182. But if the bishop should deem the paternal admonition ineffective, or if the negligent pastor should show no signs of amendment, the bishop may apply the canonical admonition of canon 2182. This canonical admonition is not to be identified with the penal remedy mentioned in canon 2307, which is given to a person who is is in the proximate occasion of committing a delict, or who is seriously suspected of having committed a grave violation of the law, but rather the strictly penal admonition of canon 2233, § 2, which presupposes with certitude the commission of a delict and invokes the threat of penalties if this delict is committed again.[6] That the strictly penal admonition is here to be understood is also apparent from the wording of canon 2182, which requires the bishop to admonish the negligent pastor by recalling to his mind both the strict obligation in conscience and the penalties inflicted for the conscious neglect of its fulfillment.[7]

Before a further step in the procedure can be taken, the pastor must be allotted a sufficient time to show that he has accepted the admonition

3. Suarez, *De Remotione Parochorum*, p. 183; Wernz-Vidal, *Ius Canonicum*, VI, 754; Coronata, *Institutiones*, III, 551.

4. Can. 2214, § 2.

5. Meier, *The Penal Administrative Procedure Against Negligent Pastors*, The Catholic University of America Canon Law Studies, n. 140 (Washington, D. C.: The Catholic University of America Press, 1941), p. 156 (hereafter cited (*Procedure Against Negligent Pastors*).

6. Meier, *Procedure Against Negligent Pastors*, p. 157.

7. Wernz-Vidal, *Ius Canonicum*, VI, 754, footnote 4; VII, 389-401; Coronata, *Institutiones*, III, 551.

and has tried to amend himself. The time limit, however, cannot definitely be set for every instance, and hence the determining of it must be left to the judgment of the bishop.[8]

Also, before the reprimand and the punishment can be applied, the bishop must have certainty that the pastor has not heeded the admonition and has continued in his grave negligence. This certainly must be possessed through reliable sources.

Moreover, the pastor should be offered an opportunity to defend himself. For the consideration of the pastor's defense, two synodial examiners should be called in by the bishop. They give a consultative vote on the matter to the bishop. After such consideration, when it has been determined that the pastor has spurned the admonition and continues in his negligence, the bishop can apply the reprimand and punishment of canon 2183.[9]

The reprimand is the penal remedy mentioned in canon 2306. It is a solemn reproof of the pastor in his failure to comply with his obligation of preaching. The reprimand must be made publicly, that is, it must be made before a notary, or two witnesses, or by means of a signed and sealed letter whose reception is assured.[10]

It is not necessary that a punishment be added to the reprimand.[11] However, if the punishment is added to the reprimand, both may be given in one and the same act.[12]

The punishment selected for the negligent pastor may be taken from the list of vindictive penalties recounted in canon 2298, or from the penal penances listed in canon 2313.[13]

Meier well observes that if some of the vindictive penalties were applied, the pastor would hardly have the chance to show amendment, since they would forbid exactly that which the pastor is obliged to do.[14] Hence some kind of penal penance would be more appropriate and would serve the purpose better.

---

8. Meier, *Procedure Against Negligent Pastors*, p. 166.

9. Wernz-Vidal, *Ius Canonicum*, VI, 754; Meier, *Procedure Against Negligent Pastors*, pp. 171-172; Suarez, *De Remotione Parochorum*, pp. 186-187; Coronata, *Institutiones*, III, 551.

10. Can. 2309.

11. Meier, *Procedure Against Negligent Pastors*, p. 179.

12 Coronata, *Institutiones*, III, 553.

13. Coronata, *Institutiones*, III, 553; Vermeersch-Creusen, *Epitome*, III, n. 371; Wernz-Vidal, *Ius Canonicum*, VI, 754.

14. Meier, *Procedure Against Negligent Pastors*, p. 180.

If the pastor should continue his negligence after the reprimand and punishment have been given, the bishop may then proceed according to canon 2184. But here again the bishop must have certitude of the continued negligence on the part of the pastor. The pastor must also be given time within which to defend himself. Again the synodal examiners together with the bishop will consider the pastor's defense. If they should judge that continued negligence is manifest, the bishop may in the case of a removable pastor deprive him immediately of his office. It is to be noted that canon 2184 uses the word *potest.* The bishop, therefore, is not obligated to deprive the removable pastor of his office at that juncture if he deems other punishments to be more effective.[15] The irremovable pastor, however, at this stage of the procedure should be deprived in whole or in part of the fruits of his benefice according to the decision of the bishop. The goods of which the pastor is deprived should be distributed among the poor.[16] Blat also maintains that the removable pastor can be deprived of the fruits of his office before he is deprived of the office itself.[17]

If the irremovable pastor after all this shows no signs of amendment, and if his contumacy has been definitely established, the bishop must proceed to the decree of removal from office or benefice, according to canon 2185. Under the postulated conditions the irremovable pastor must be removed from his office or benefice, since the law uses the preceptive word *removeat.* [18]

Against the decree of removal from office the pastor, whether removable or irremovable, may within ten days invoke a recourse to the Holy See, that is, to the Sacred Congregation of the Council, or to the Sacred Congregation for the Propagation of the Faith, or to the Sacred Congregation entrusted with the affairs of Religious, as the case demands. This recourse has no suspensive effect; hence the pastor must obey the decree of the bishop during the time the recourse is pending.[19]

---

15. Coronata, *Institutiones,* III, 554; Meier, *Procedure Against Negligent Pastors,* p. 185.
16. Can. 2184.
17. Blat, *Commentarium,* Lib. IV, 702.
18. Woywod, "Procedural Law of the Code: Procedure Against a Pastor Negligent in the Fulfillment of his Pastoral Duties," *HPR,* XXXV (1935), 951-953.
19. Coronata, *Institutiones,* III, 555; Wernz-Vidal, *Ius Canonicum,* VI, 755; Meier, *Procedure Against Negligent Pastors,* p. 197.

During the pending of the recourse the law requires the ordinary to place a substitute vicar in the parish or benefice.[20]

This penal administrative procedure can be used not only against negligent pastors in the strict sense, but also against all those who come under the name of pastors in the law. Such are the quasi-pastors and the parochial vicars who are endowed with full parochial powers.[21] The following clerics are therefore subject to this process: 1) pastors in the strict sense; 2) quasi-pastors if they are of the secular clergy;[22] 3) parochial vicars who are endowed with complete parochial powers and 4) those assistant pastors (*vicarii cooperatores*) who have a benefice.[23] Cases of the latter are likely to exist only in Europe.[24]

Other parochial vicars, such as the vicar econome, the substitute vicar, the adjutant, and the assistant, have only temporary appointments and lack true stability. Even though such parochial vicars may have the same obligations as those of a pastor during their incumbency, nevertheless they are not removed from office according to this penal procedure for negligence on their part. They are removed from office simply at the equitable discretion of the local ordinary.[25] However, all of these can be punished for negligence in the performance of their duties. Applicable are the penal remedies and the penances mentioned in canon 2313.

McVann is of the opinion that a serious violation of the law of canon 1345 also leaves room for the application of canon 2382. Consequently the pastor who is negligent in regard to the prescriptions of canon 1345 could likewise be subjected to this penal administrative procedure.[26] Meier contradicts this opinion.[27] The writer agrees with the opinion of Meier. None of the authors bring the violation of the law of canon 1345 within the penal scope of canon 2382. Furthermore, canon 1345, as expressed in the Code, evinces a strong desire rather than a legislative demand, and hence does not place any strict obligation on the priests to

---

20. Can. 2146.
21. Can. 451, § 2.
22. Pastors and quasi-pastors of the religious or regular clergy are not mentioned here as coming under this process because they are removable *ad nutum loci ordinarii*. Cf. can. 454, § 5.
23. Can. 477, § 2.
24. Meier, *Procedure Against Negligent Pastors*, p. 121.
25. Can. 477, § 1.
26. McVann, *The Canon Law on Sermon Preaching*, pp. 122-123.
27. Meier, *Procedure Against Negligent Pastors*, p. 146.

preach until the ordinary has so legislated through particular law. Consequently, since there is not any strict obligation expressed in canon 1345, there also is no specified punishment which serves as an especial penal sanction for the observance of what this canon evinces as the lawgiver's desire.[28]

If the local ordinary by particular law places a strict obligation on priests to preach under the circumstances contemplated in canon 1345, what then may be the procedure against priests who are negligent? At first glance there seems to be no manner of procedure. But even if the local ordinary has not fortified the observance of his own particular law by means of penal sanctions, he may nevertheless use the penal remedies and the penal penances against those who prove negligent.[29]

Moreover, the local ordinary could apply canon 2399 against a priest who is negligent in regard to canon 1345. Canon. 2399 invokes a penal sanctions for the proper observance of canon 128, which prescribes that as often and as long as in the judgment of the ordinary the necessity of the Church demands it, the cleric must accept and faithfully fulfill the duty committed to him by the ordinary, unless he is excused by a legitimate impediment. *Munus* is understood as any kind of office in the wide sense,[30] which accordingly also includes preaching. The ordinary can punish any wilful negligence in or desertion from the duties implied in such an office by means of a suspenson *a divinis.* This punishment is a vindictive *ferendae sententiae* penalty. The ordinary, however, can inflict this punishment by means of a precept apart from the need of any previous judicial process.[31]

Furthermore, if the ordinary has placed a strict obligation on pastors to preach under the conditions envisioned in canon 1345, the pastor who then is negligent in this matter can easily render his ministry harmful and inefficacious. Hence he could be removed from office according to the regular administrative procedure of removal as expressed in canons 2147-2156 and canons 2157-2167.[32]

28. Coronata, *Institutiones*, IV, 3-5.
29. Coronata, *Institutiones*, IV, 276; 285-286.
30. Can. 145, § 1; Coronata, *Institutiones*, IV, 675.
31. Can. 1933, § 4; Coronata, *Institutiones*, IV, 675.
32. Meier, *Procedure Against Negligent Pastors*, p. 146.

ARTICLE 2. *Other Penalties with Reference to the Neglect of Preaching*

In the *Norms for Sacred Preaching* the Sacred Consistorial Congregation set down the rules for the material content of the sermon and the manner of delivery.[33]

It determined further that those who are negligent in following these prescriptions, if the offense is not grave and they give hope of amendment, may for the first and second time be warned and reprimanded by the bishop. But if they fail to amend, or if their offense was grave inasmuch as it occasioned scandal to the faithful, the bishop shall revoke the permission to preach either temporarily or permanently if the priest is his own subject or a religious to whom he has given permission; if the priest in question is from outside the diocese or a religious who did not obtain the permission from the local ordinary, the bishop shall forbid such a priest to preach in his diocese and issue notice of that effect to the respective ordinaries.[34]

The bishop should also forbid preaching at least temporarily and with reference to certain places to anyone who by his manner of life or for any other reason, even without his fault, has lost his good reputation before the public, so that his ministry has become useless or harmful.[35]

On the other hand, where the priest is at fault or has committed a delict, applicable are the vindictive penalties of canon 2298, 1°, which prohibits priests the exercise of a sacred duty except in a determined church, and of canon 2299, § 2, which forbids the priest to exercise the office of preaching for a specified length of time.

Those preachers who knowingly and wilfully, whether privately or publicly, teach and disseminate doctrine which is not formally heretical, but which has been condemned by the Apostolic See or by a General Council, are to be prohibited from exercising the office of preaching, the office of hearing confessions, and any other office of teaching. The condemnatory sentence may include other punishments, and the ordinary,

33. S.C. Consist., *Ut quae,* 28 iun. 1917, nn. 19-28—Bouscaren, The Canon Law *Digest,* I, 627-628.

34. S.C. Consist., *Ut quae,* 28 iun. 1917, nn. 29-30—Bouscaren, *The Canon Law Digest,* I, 628-629.

35. S.C. Consist., *Ut quae,* 28 iun. 1917, n. 31—Bouscaren, *The Canon Law Digest,* I, 629; Ayrinhac, *Administrative Legislation,* p. 229.

after an unheeded admonition, may inflict other punishments to repair the scandal done.[36]

Preachers who disseminate heresy are punished according to canons 2314 and 2315.[37]

According to canon 2314 heretics are *ipso facto* excommunicated. Absolution from this excommunication is reserved to the Holy See in a special manner. If, after being admonished, they continue in error, they should be deprived of all offices, benefices and dignities, declared infamous, and, if they be clerics, they shall after a second fruitless admonition be deposed.[38] All these punishments except the excommunication are of a *ferendae sententiae* character.

Those clerics who are suspected of heresy after an admonition has twice been repeated without the desired effect are to be suspended *a divinis*; and if thereafter no amendment is made within six months, such a one is to be considered as a heretic, liable to the punishments of a heretic.[39]

The Sacred Consistorial Congregation in its *Norms for Sacred Preaching* gave local ordinaries the right to prescribe that their clerics shall, for a certain number of years, undergo every year in the curia an oral and written examination in preaching, in whatever way they deem best, conformably to the prescriptions of the Code as regards the annual examinations of clerics after their ordination to the priesthood.[40]

Canon 130 requires yearly examinations for a term of at least three years after the completion of a priest's theological studies in all the sacred sciences, namely, in dogmatic, moral, pastoral, ascetical and mystical theology, in liturgy, in church history, in Sacred Scripture, in canon law, in sacred eloquence, in homiletics, and in catechetics. It belongs to the local ordinary to determine the particular matter, the time, the place, and the examiners for the examination.[41]

The III Plenary Council of Baltimore decreed that such examinations should be held annually for five years after the ordination to the priest-

36. Can. 2317.
37. Can. 1347, § 3.
38. Can. 2314.
39. Can. 2315.
40. S.C. Consist., *Ut quae,* 28 iun. 1917, n. 40—Bouscaren, *The Canon Law Digest,* I, 630.
41. Coronata, *Institutiones,* I, 220.

hood.[42] Since this decree of the council touches a matter that remains outside the common law, it is still in force.[43]

Those priests who refuse to take the examinations prescribed by canon 130 shall be compelled by means of suitable penalties to do so.[44] It is of course postulated that their refusal is of a positive character. But if the time, place and matter of the examination have been made known, the very failure to appear at the examination in the absence of any legitimate excuse would suffice to demonstrate such a refusal.[45]

The punishments adverted to in canon 2376 are not of a determinate character, that is, the specific penalties to be employed are optional, but they are preceptive for their infliction. Except in cases of protracted stubbornness, however, censures should not be used.[46]

There is question whether canon 2376 can be applied to n. 40 of the *Norms*. In so far as n. 40 of the *Norms* is incorporated in canon 130, the penalties of canon 2376 can be applied. But when the further import of n. 40 of the *Norms* has been constituted as particular law, then the ordinary can proceed against negligence by means of a precept which carries the threat of punishment.

Moreover, the infliction of the penalties resting within the local ordinary's option according to canon 2376 seems inapplicable if a priest refuses to take the examinations for the two extra years as required by the III Plenary Council of Baltimore. But there again the ordinary could proceed against the delinquent by means of a precept fortified with the threat of punishment.[47]

Besides the fact that the III Plenary Council of Baltimore required the ordinary to punish severely those who obstinately neglect to preach a sermon at every Mass on Sundays and feast days,[48] the writer has not been able to find any other enacted penalties in the particular law with reference to the culpable neglect of preaching.

It remains only to determine whether an excommunicated, suspended or irregular priest may preach.

---

42. *Acta et Decreta Conc. Balt. III*, n. 187.
43. Beste, *Introductio in Codicem*, p. 185.
44. Can. 2376.
45. Augustine, *A Commentary*, VIII, 454-455.
46. Can. 2241, § 2; Augustine, *A Commentary*, VIII, 454-455; Coronata, *Institutiones*, IV, 643.
47. Can. 2233.
48. *Acta et Decreta Conc. Balt. III*, n. 215.

Canon 2263 prohibits the excommunicated priest from performing any ecclesiastical office or duty. Here the ecclesiastical office is understood in the wide sense as well as in the strict sense.[49] Included under the ecclesiastical office in the wide sense is the office of preaching.[50]

The priest who is suspended from his office (*ab officio*) is deprived also of the faculty of preaching, for he is forbidden to exercise any and every act stemming from the power of orders and jurisdiction as well as every act of mere administration of which he is competent by reason of his office.[51] Preaching may not be considered as an act of the powers of orders or of jurisdiction, but certainly it can be included among the acts of mere administration of which the priest is competent by reason of his office.

The priest who is suspended from jurisdiction (*a jurisdictione*) may preach. This suspension forbids the performance of any act which requires the power of jurisdiction.[52] But since preaching is an act of administration which has been attached to an office or delegated to a person, it is not included among those acts which are forbidden by this suspension.

The priest who is irregular is not thereby prohibited from preaching. Irregularity is an impediment which, by the positive law of the Church, perpetually prohibits the conferral and reception and the exercise of holy orders on account of the reverence of the divine ministry.[53] Consequently, even though sacred orders may be the foundation for the authorization to preach, nevertheless preaching itself is not precisely an act of orders.

---

49. Can. 145, § 1.
50. Beste, *Introductio in Codicem*, p. 199; Coronata, *Institutiones*, IV, 212.
51. Can. 2279, § 1; Beste, *Introductio in Codicem*, p. 946.
52. Can. 2279, § 2, 1°; Coronata, *Institutiones*, IV, 247.
53. Coronata, *Institutiones Iuris Canonici, De Sacramentis Tractatus Canonicus* (3 vols., Taurini, Romae: Domus Editorialis Marietti, 1943-1945), II, 121.

CONCLUSIONS

1. Superiors of clerical exempt religious Orders should not subject a diocesan priest who is approved for preaching by his own local ordinary to an examination before they grant him the faculty to preach to their own subjects.

2. Pastors, even though in virtue of their pastoral office they have all needed authorization for preaching, cannot delegate the faculty of preaching unless the power of delegation has been granted to them by particular law.

3. Lay men or lay women who give catechetical instructions, whether in or outside of school, do not and can not receive the canonical commission. However, this instructing should be given under episcopal supervision.

4. Particular law should determine the manner in which the twofold obligation of preaching a homily and of giving catechetical instructions should be fulfilled on Sundays and feast days.

5. Sermons are required at every Mass on Sundays and feast days, even during the summertime, by the law of the III Plenary Council of Baltimore, which still has binding force. Bishops, however, can dispense from this law on particular occasions and for a just cause.

6. The penal administrative procedure for removal from office can be used against the pastor, and one who according to the law comes under the name of pastor, only if he has been negligent in the duty of preaching for three continuous months.

BIBLIOGRAPHY

Sources

Acta Apostolicae Sedis, Commentarium Officiale, Romae, 1909 ——.

Acta et Decreta Concilii Plenarii Baltimorensis Tertii, A.D. MDCCCLXXXIV, Baltimorae: John Murphy, 1886.

Acta et Decreta Concilii Provincialis Portlandensis in Oregon Quarti, diebus VIII, IX, X, Septembris 1932 habiti, Portland, Oregon: Sentinel Printery, 1934.

Acta et Decreta Sacrorum Conciliorum Recentiorum, Collectio Lacensis, 7 vols., Friburgi Brisgoviae, 1870-1892.

Acta et Decreta Synodi Dioecesanae Quebecensis Secundae, a. 1940, Quebeci: Cancellaria Curiae Metropolitanae, 1940.

Acta et Decreta Synodi Dioecesanae Toletanae Primae, a. 1941, Toleti: Cancellaria Curiae Dioecesanae, 1941.

Acta Sanctae Sedis, 41 vols., Romae, 1865-1908.

Bouscaren, T. L., *The Canon Law Digest,* 2 vols., Milwaukee: Bruce, 1934-1943.

Bullarum Diplomatum et Privilegiorum Sanctorum Romanorum Pontificum Taurinensis Editio, 24 vols. et Appendix, Augustae Taurinorum, 1857-1872.

Canones Apostolorum et Conciliorum Saeculorum IV-VIII, ed. H. T. Bruns, 2 vols., Berolini, 1839.

Canones et Decreta Sacrosancti Oecumenici Concilii Tridentini, Editio novissima ad Fidem Optimorum Exemplarium Castigate Impressa (XIX reimpressio stereotypa), Taurini, 1913.

Code of the Diocese of Des Moines decreed in Diocesan Synod, held June 15, 1923, and promulgated September 8, 1923.

Codex Iuris Canonici Pii X Pontificis Maximi iussu digestus, Benedicti Papae XV auctoritate promulgatus, Romae: Typis Polyglottis Vaticanis, 1917.

Codicis Iuris Canonici Fontes, cura Emi Petri Card. Gasparri editi, 9 vols., Romae (postea Civitate Vaticana): Typis Polyglottis Vaticanis, 1923-1939. Vols. VII-IX, ed. cura et studio Emi Iustiniani Card. Seredi.

Collectanea S. Congregationis de Propaganda Fide, 2 vols., Romae: Typographia Polyglotta S.C. de Propaganda Fide, 1907.

Constitutiones Dioecesos Sinus Viridis quae in Synodo Dioecesana Quarta diebus 14-15-16 Decembris 1920 habita, latae et promulgatae fuerunt, Pulaski, Wisc.: Typhis Franciscanae Typographiae, 1921.

Corpus Iuris Canonici, editio Lipsiensis secunda, post Aemilii Ludovici Richteri curas instruxit Aemilius Friedberg, 2 vols., Lipsiae, 1879-1881. Editio anastatice repetita, Lipsiae: Tauchnitz, 1928.

Decreta Authentica Congregationis Sacrorum Rituum, 6 vols., Romae: Ex Typographia Polyglotta, 1898-1927.

Decretales D. Gregorii Papae IX, una cum glossis restitutae, 2 vols., Romae, 1582.

Decretum Gratiani emendatum et notationibus illustratum una cum glossis, 3 vols., Romae, 1582.

Hardouin, Jean, *Acta Conciliorum et Epistolae Decretales ac Constitutiones Summorum Pontificum*, 12 vols., Parisiis, 1714-1715.

Jaffe, Philippus, *Regesta Pontificum Romanorum ab condita Ecclesia ad annum post Christum natum MCXCVIII*, 2 ed., cura G. Wattenbach, F. Kaltenbrunner (ad annum 590), P. Ewald (anno 590-882), S. Loewenfeld (anno 882-1198), 2 vols., Lipsiae, 1885-1888.

Mansi, Joannes, *Sacrorum Conciliorum Nova et Amplissima Collectio*, 53 vols. in 60, Parisiis, 1901-1927.

Missale Romanum, Editio XIV iuxta Typicam Vaticanam, Ratisbonae: Sumptibus et Typis Friderici Pustet, 1930.

Monumenta Germaniae Historica, 188 vols. incomplete, Hannoverae, 1826 ——, Legum Sectio II, *Capitularia Regum Francorum*, Tom. I, ed. A. Boretius, 1883; *Scriptores*, Tom. IV, ed. G. Petrz, 1841.

Pallottini, Salvator, *Collectio Omnium Conclusionum et Resolutionum Quae in Causis Propositis apud Sacram Congregationem Cardinalium S. Concilii Tridentini Interpretum Prodierunt ab eius Institutione anno MDLXIV ad annum MDCCCLX, distin tis titulis alphabetico ordine per materias digesta*, 18 vols., Romae, 1868-1893.

Pontificale Romanum, Summorum Pontificum iussu editum, a Benedicto XIV et Leone XIII Pont. Max. recognitum et castigatum, Ratisbonae, 1908.

Potthast, Augustus, *Regesta Pontificum Romanorum inde ab anno post Christum natum MCXCVIII ad annum MCCCIV*, 2 vols., Berolini, 1874-1875.

Schroeder, H. J., *Canons and Decrees of the Council of Trent, Original Text with English Translation*, St. Louis, Mo.: B. Herder Book Co., 1941.

Statuta Dioecesis Lacus Salsi lata et promulgata in Synodo Dioecesana Prima, die 17 Junii 1929 habita, Bronx, N. Y.: New York Catholic Protectory, 1929.

Statuta Dioecesis Montereyensis-Fresnensis in Prima Synodo Dioecesana, diebus 29 et 30 Octobris 1929 lata et promulgata, Fresni: Sumptibus Saint Columba Guild, 1929.

Statuta Dioeceseos Pittsburgensis in Synodo Dioecesana XIV lata, die 8 O tobris 1919, Pittsburgh, Pa.: St. Joseph's Protectory Print, 1920.

Statuta Synodi Altunensis Primae, III Kal. Decembris MCMXXII, Lancaster, Pa.: Wickersham Printing Co., 1923.

Synodus Dioecesana Buffalensis Vigesima Septima, die 14 Maii 1924, Buffalo, N. Y.: Union and Times Press, 1924.

Synodus Dioecesana Fargensis Prima, diebus XXIX et XXX Septembris, A.D. 1941 habita, Milwauchiae: Ex Typographia Bruce, 1941.

Synodus Dioecesana Philadelphiensis IX, habita die vigesima sexta Aprilis, A.D. 1934, in Sacello Sti. Martini, Overbrook.

Synodus Dioecesis Richmondiensis Tertia, die 16 Februarii 1933 celebrata, Richmond, Va.: Lewis Printing Co., 1933.

Synodus Dioecesana Syracusensis Undecima, die XVIII Septembris 1921 habita, Rochester, N. Y.: Typis Joannis P. Smith Printing Co., 1922.

AUTHORS

Aertnys, J. - Damen, C. A., *Theologia Moralis,* 14. ed., 2 vols., Taurini: Marietti, 1944.

Aquinas, St. Thomas, *Summa Theologica,* 6 vols., Taurini, Romae: Marietti, 1937.

Augustine, Charles, *A Commentary on the New Code of Canon Law,* 3. ed., 8 vols., St. Louis, Mo.: B. Herder Book Co., 1919-1931.

Ayrinhac, H. A., *Administrative Legislation of the New Code of Canon Law,* London, New York, Toronto: Longmans, Green & Co., 1930.

Ballerini, A. - Palmieri, D., *Opus Theologicum Morale,* 7 vols., Prati, 1889-1893.

Barbosa, Augustinus, *Pastoralis Solicitudinis sive de Officio et Potestate Parochi Tripartita Descriptio,* 5. ed., Lugduni, 1665.

Bargilliat, Michael, *Praelectiones Juris Canonici,* 37. ed., 2 vols., Parisiis: Baston, Berche et Pagis, 1923.

Benedictus XIV (Prosper Lambertini), *De Synodo Dioecesana,* 2 vols., Romae, 1806.

Berardi, Aemilius, *De Parocho Compendium,* Faventiae: Ex Typographia Novelli, 1887.

Berengo, Joannes, *Enchiridion Parochorum seu Institutiones Theologiae Pastoralis,* 2. ed., Venetiis, 1877.

Berutti, Christophorus, *Institutiones Iuris Canonici,* 6 vols., Vol. IV, Taurini, Romae: Marietti, 1940.

Beste, Udalricus, *Introductio in Codicem,* 3. ed., Collegeville, Minn.: St. John's Abbey Press, 1946.

Blat, Albertus, *Commentarium Textus Codicis Iuris Canonici,* 5 vols. in 6, Romae: Ex Typographia Pontificia in Instituto Pii X, 1919-1927.

Bouix, Dominicus, *Tractatus de Parocho,* 3. ed., Parisiis, 1880.

Bouscaren, T. L. - Ellis, A. C., *Canon Law, A Text and Commentary,* Milwaukee: Bruce Publishing Co., 1946.

Cappello, Felix, *Summa Iuris Canonici,* 3 vols., Vols. I-II, 4. ed., 1945; Vol. III, 2. ed., 1940, Romae: Apud Aedes Universitatis Gregorianae.

Chelodi, Joannes, *Ius Canonicum de Personis,* 3. ed. curavit Pius Ciprotti, Vicenza: Societa Anonima Tipografica, 1942.

Claeys-Bouuaert, F. - Simenon, G., *Manuale Juris Canonici,* 3 vols., Vols. I et III, 3. ed., 1930; Vol. II, 1931, Gandae et Leodii: H. Dessain.

Cocchi, Guidus, *Commentarium in Codicem Iuris Canonici,* 8 vols. in 5, Vol. I, 5. ed., 1938; Vol. II, 4. ed., 1937; Vol. III, 3. ed., 1932; Vol. IV, 4. ed., 1942; Vol. V, 4. ed., 1942; Vol. VI, 3. ed., 1933; Vol. VII, 3. ed., 1940; Vol. VIII, 4. ed., 1938, Taurini: Marietti.

Connolly, Nicholas, *The Canonical Erection of Parishes,* The Catholic University of America Canon Law Studies, n. 114, Washington, D. C.: The Catholic University of America, 1938.

Coronata, Matthaeus Conte a, *Institutiones Iuris Canonici,* ed. altera, 5 vols., Taurini: Marietti, 1939-1946.

——————, *Institutiones Iuris Canonici, De Sacramentis Tractatus Canonicus,* 3 vols., Taurini: Marietti, 1943-1946.

Dargan, Edwin C., *A History of Preaching*, New York: A. C. Armstrong & Son, 1905.

De Meester, Alfonsus, *Juris Canonici et Juris Canonico-civilis Compendium*, nova ed., 3 vols. in 4, Brugis: Desclee de Brouwer, 1921-1928.

Dictionnaire de Theologie Catholique, ed. E. Vacant (1901), E. Mangenot (1922), and E. Amann (1880-1948), 28 vols. incomplete, Paris: Letouzey et Ane, 1903-1946.

Drumm, William, *Hospital Chaplains*, The Catholic University of America Canon Law Studies, n. 178, Washington, D. C.: The Catholic University of America Press, 1943.

Fagnanus, Prosper, *Commentaria in Quinque Libros Decretalium*, 5 vols. in 4, Venetiis, 1709.

Fanfani, Ludovicus, *De Iure Parochorum*, Taurini, Romae: Marietti, 1924.

Feldhaus, Aloysius, *Oratories*, The Catholic University of America Canon Law Studies, n. 42, Washington, D. C.: The Catholic University of America, 1927.

Ferraris, Lucius, *Prompta Bibliotheca Canonica, Iuridica, Moralis, Theologica, necnon Ascetica, Polemica, Rubricistica, Historica*, ed. noviss., 9 vols., Romae, 1885-1899.

Funk, Franciscus X., *Didascalia et Constitutiones Apostolorum*, 2 vols., Paderbornae, 1905.

Giraldi, Ubaldus, *Expositio Iuris Pontificii*, 2 vols., Romae, 1829-1830.

Haring, J. B., *Grundzuege des katholischen Kirchenrechtes*, 3. ed., 2 vols., Graz: Ulrich Mosers Buchhandlung, 1924.

Hefele, Carolus - LeClercq, Henri, *Histoire des Conciles*, 10 vols. in 19, Paris: Letouzey et Ane, 1907-1938.

Heimbucher, Max Joseph, *Die Orden und Kongregationen der katholischen Kirche*, 3. ed., 2 vols., Paderborn: Verlag Ferdinand Schoningh, 1933-1934.

Herve, Jean Marie, *Manuale Theologiae Dogmaticae*, 4 vols., Vol. I, 19. ed.; Vol. II, 17. ed.; Vol. III, 18. ed.; Vol. IV, 16. ed., Westminster, Md.: The Newman Bookshop, 1943.

Hinschius, Paul, *Das Kirchenrecht der Katholiken und Protestanten in Deutschland*, 6 vols., Berlin, 1869-1897.

Hollweck, Joseph, *Die kirchlichen Strafgesetze*, Mainz, 1899.

Hostiensis, Cardinalis (Henricus de Segusia), *Commentaria in Quinque Libros Decretalium*, 5 vols. in 3, Venetiis, 1581.

Jansen, Raymond, *Canonical Provisions for Catechetical Instruction*, The Catholic University of American Canon Law Studies, n. 107, Washington, D. C.: The Catholic University of America, 1937.

Koudelka, Charles, *Pastors, Their Rights and Duties according to the New Code of Canon Law*, The Catholic University of America Canon Law Studies, n. 11, Washington, D. C.: The Catholic University of America, 1921.

Lehmkuhl, Augustinus, *Theologia Moralis*, 9. ed., 2 vols., Friburgi Brisgoviae: Herder, 1898-1899.

Liguori, St. Alphonsus, *Theologia Moralis*, ed. accuratior, 2 vols., Augustae Taurinorum: Ex Typis Hyacinthi Marietti, 1879.

McVann, James, *The Canon Law on Sermon Preaching*, New York: The Paulist Press, 1940.

Meier, Carl, *Penal Administrative Procedure Against Negligent Pastors*, The Catholic University of America Canon Law Studies, n. 140, Washington, D. C.: The Catholic University of America Press, 1941.

Migne, J. P., *Patrologiae Cursus Completus, Series Latina*, 221 vols., Parisiis, 1844-1864.

Moersdorf, Klaus, *Die Rechtssprache des Codex Iuris Canonici*, Paderborn: Verlag Ferdinand Schoningh, 1937.

Motry, H. L., *Diocesan Faculties according to the Code of Canon Law*, The Catholic University of America Canon Law Studies, n. 16, Washington, D. C.: The Catholic University of America, 1922.

Mueller, Ewald, *Das Konzil von Vienne* 1311-1312, *Seine Quellen und seine Geschichte*, Muenster in Westfalen; Verlag Aschendorff, 1934.

New English Dictionary on Historical Principles, ed. James A. H. Murray and H. Bradley, Oxford: The Clarendon Press, 1888-1928.

Ojetti, Benedictus, *Synopsis Rerum Moralium et Iuris Pontificii*, 3. ed., 3 vols. et. Index, Romae: 1909-1914.

Pignatelli, Jacobus, *Consultationes Canonicae*, 10 vols. in 5, Coloniae Allobrogorum, 1700.

Pruemmer, Dominicus, *Manuale Iuris Canonici*, 6. ed., Friburgi Brisgoviae: Herder, 1933.

Realencyklopaedie fuer protestantische Theologie und Kirche, 3. ed., ed. A. Hauck, 24 vols., Leipzig, 1896-1913.

Regatillo, Eduardus, *Institutiones Iuris Canonici*, 2 vols., Vol. I, 1946; Vol. II, 1942, Santander: Sal Terrae.

Reiffenstuel, Anacletus, *Ius Canonicum Universum*, 7 vols., Parisiis, 1864-1870.

Rossi, Josephus, *De Paroecia, iuxta Codicem Iuris Canonici*, Romae: Pustet, 1923.

Saegmueller, J. B., *Lehrbuch des katholischen Kirchenrechts*, 3 vols. in 1, Freiburg im Breisgau: Herder, 1900-1904.

Scavini, Petrus, *Theologia Moralis Universa*, 11. ed., 4 vols., Mediolani, 1869.

Schaefer, Timotheus, *De Religiosis ad Normam Codicis Iuris Canonici*, 3. ed. aucta et emendata, Roma: Herder, 1940.

Scherer, Rudolph, Ritter von, *Handbuch des Kirchenrechtes*, 2 vols., Graz, 1886-1898.

Schleininger, Nikolaus, *Das kirchliche Predigtamt*, 3. ed., Freiburg im Breisgau: Herder, 1881.

Schmalzgrueber, Franciscus, *Ius Ecclesiasticum Universum*, 5 vols. in 12, Romae, 1843-1845.

Schroeder, H. J., *Disciplinary Decrees of the General Councils, Text, Translation and Commentary*, St. Louis, Mo.: B. Herder Book Co., 1937.

Sipos, Stephanus, *Enchiridion Iuris Canonici*, 3. ed., Pecs: Ex Typographia "Haladas R. T.," 1936.

Suarez, Emmanuel, *De Remotione Parochorum*, Romae: Pontificium Internationale Institutum "Angelicum" de Urbe, 1931.

Suarez, Franciscus, *Opera Omnia*, 28 vols., Parisiis: Apud Ludovicum Vives, 1856-1878.

Tanquerey, A., *Synopsis Theologiae Moralis et Pastoralis*, 3 vols., Vol. I, 11. ed., 1930; Vols. II-III, 9. ed., 1930-1931, Parisiis, Tornaci, Romae: Desclee et Socii.

Thomassinus, Ludovicus, *Vetus et Nova Disciplina circa Beneficia et Beneficiarios*, 10 vols., Magontiaci, 1787.

Toso, A., *Ad Codicem Iuris Canonici Commentaria Minora*, 5 vols., Vol. I, 2. ed., 1921; Vols. II-V, 1922-1927, Romae: Marietti.

Vermeersch, Arturus, *Theologiae Moralis Principia, Responsa, Concilia*, 3. ed., 4 vols., Romae: Universita Gregoriana, 1933-1937.

Vermeersch, Arturus - Creusen, Josephus, *Epitome Iuris Canonici*, 6. ed., 3 vols., Romae: Dessain, 1937-1946.

Wagner, Urban, *Parochial Substitute Vicars and Supplying Priests*, The Catholic University of America Canon Law Studies, n. 265, Washington, D. C.: The Catholic University of America Press, 1947.

Wernz, Franciscus X., *Ius Decretalium*, 2. ed., 6 vols., Romae et Prati, 1906-1913.

Wernz, Franciscus X. - Vidal, Petrus, *Ius Canonicum*, 7 vols. in 8, Romae: Apud Aedes Universitatis Gregorianae, 1923-1938.

Woywod, Stanislaus, *A Practical Commentary on the Code of Canon Law*, 9. ed., 2 vols. (revised by Rev. Callistus Smith, O.F.M.), New York: Joseph F. Wagner, Inc., 1945.

Articles

Hellmuth, Hugo, "Die Missio Canonica," *Archiv fuer katholisches Kirchenrecht*, XCI (1911), 450-476.

Hofmann, Michael, "Recensionen," *Zeitschrift fuer katholische Theologie*, XXIII (1899), 703.

MacCarthy, Joseph, "The New Regulations on Preaching," *The Ecclesiastical Review*, LVII (1917), 377-389.

Park, Charles E., "The Necessity of Installation of Pastors," *The Homiletic and Pastoral Review*, XXXV (1395), 579-592.

Schaaf, V., "Corporal Installation of Pastors," *The Ecclesiastical Review*, XCI (1934), 620-624.

Snee, J. M. - Clark, J. D., "Synthesis of the Diocesan Faculties in the United States," *Theological Studies*, IX (1948), 351; 375-377.

Woywod, S., "Procedural Law of the Code: Procedure Against a Pastor Negligent in the Fulfillment of his Pastoral Duties," *The Homiletic and Pastoral Review*, XXXV (1935), 951-953.

PERIODICALS

Archiv fuer katholisches Kirchenrecht, Innsbruck, 1857-1861; Mainz, 1862 —
American Ecclesiastical Review, The, (from July 1905 to December 1943, *The Ecclesiastical Review*), Philadelphia, 1889-1943; Washington, D. C., 1944 —

Homiletic and Pastoral Review, The, New York, 1900 —

Theological Studies, Woodstock, Md., 1940 —

Zeitschrift fuer katholische Theologie, Innsbruck, 1877 —

ABBREVIATIONS

AAS—Acta Apostolicae Sedis.
ASS—Acta Sanctae Sedis.
Bruns—*Canones Apostolorum et Conciliorum IV-VII Saeculorum*, ed. H. T. Bruns.
Bull. Rom.—*Bullarum Diplomatum et Privilegiorum Sanctorum Pontificum Taurinensis Editio.*
C.—Causa.
c.—canon seu caput (iuris antiqui).
cc.—canones set capita (iuris antiqui).
can.—canon (novi Codicis).
cans.—canones (novi Codicis).
Coll. Lac.—*Acta et Decreta Sacrorum Conciliorum Recentiorum, Collectio Lacensis.*
Conc. Trident.—Concilium Tridentinum.
D.—Distinctio (iuris antiqui).
DA—*Decreta Authentica Congregationis Sacrorum Rituum.*
Fontes—*Codicis Iuris Canonici Fontes*, cura . . . Gasparri ed.
Hardouin—*Acta Conciliorum etc.*
HPR—*The Homiletic and Pastoral Review.*
JE—Jaffe, *Regesta Pontificum Romanorum etc.* (edited by P. Ewald; for the years 590-882).
JK—Jaffe, *op. cit.* (edited by F. Kaltenbrunner; to the year 590).
JL—Jaffe, *op. cit.* (edited by S. Loewenfeld; for the years 882-1198).
Mansi—*Sacrorum Conciliorum Nova et Amplissima Collectio.*
MGH—*Monumenta Germaniae Historica.*
Potthast—*Regesta Pontificum . . . . ab . . MCXCVIII ad MCCCIV.*
S.C.C.—Sacra Congregatio Concilii.
S.C.Consist.—Sacra Congregatio Consistorialis.
S.C. de Prop. Fide—Sacra Congregatio de Propaganda Fide.
S.C. Ep. et Reg.—Sacra Congregatio Episcoporum et Regul.
S.R.C.—Sacrorum Rituum Congregatio.

ALPHABETICAL INDEX

BIOGRAPHICAL NOTE

Joseph L. Allgeier was born on October 2, 1913, in Buechel, Kentucky. His elementary education he received at St. Agnes and St. James Parochial Schools in Louisville. He attended high school and college at St. Joseph's College, Collegeville, Indiana. The philosophical and theological studies he made at the Imperial University of Innsbruck, Austria, and at the Facultas Theologica Oenipontana-Sedunensis in Sion, Switzerland. He was ordained to the priesthood in Sion, Switzerland, March 23, 1940, for service in the Archdiocese of Louisville. After serving as assistant in the parish of St. Therese, Louisville, he entered the Graduate School of Canon Law at the Catholic University of America in September, 1946. From this School he received the degree of the Baccalaureate in Canon Law in June, 1947, and that of the Licentiate in Canon Law in June, 1948.

CANON LAW STUDIES*

1. Freriks, Rev. Celestine A., C. PP. S., J. C. D., Religious Congregations in Their External Relations, 121 pp., 1916.
2. Galliher, Rev. Daniel M., O. P., J. C. D., Canonical Elections, 117 pp., 1917.
3. Borkowski, Rev. Aurelius L., O. F. M., J. C. D., De Confraternitatibus Ecclesiasticis, 136 pp., 1918.
4. Castillo, Rev. Cayo, J. C. D., Disertacion Historico-Canonica sobre la Potestad del Cabildo en Sede Vacante o Impedida del Vicario Capitular, 99 pp., 1919 (1918).
5. Kubelbeck, Rev. William J., S. T. B., J. C. D., The Sacred Penitentiaria and Its Relation to Faculties of Ordinaries and Priests, 129 pp., 1918.
6. Petrovits, Rev. Joseph, J. C., S. T. D., J. C. D., The New Church Law on Matrimony, X-461 pp., 1919.
7. Hickey, Rev. John J., S. T. B., J. C. D., Irregularities and Simple Impediments in the New Code of Canon Law, 100 pp., 1920.
8. Klekotka, Rev. Peter J., S. T. B., J. C. D., Diocesan Consultors, 179 pp., 1920.
9. Wanenmacher, Rev. Francis, J. C. D., The Evidence in Ecclesiastical Procedure Affecting the Marriage Bond, 1920 (Printed 1935).
10. Golden, Rev. Henry Francis, J. C. D., Parochial Benefices in the New Code, IV-119 pp., 1921 (Printed 1925).
11. Koudelka, Rev. Charles J., J. C. D., Pastors, Their Rights and Duties According to the New Code of Canon Law, 211 pp., 1921.
12. Melo, Rev. Antonius, O. F. M., J. C. D., De Exemptione Regularium, X-188 pp., 1921.
13. Schaaf, Rev. Valentine Theodore, O. F. M., S. T. B., J. C. D., The Cloister, X-180 pp., 1921.
14. Burke, Rev. Thomas Joseph, S. T. D., J. C. D., Competence in Ecclesiastical Tribunals, IV-117 pp., 1922.
15. Leech, Rev. George Leo, J. C. D., A Comparative Study of the Constitution "Apostolicae Sedis" and the "Codex Juris Canonici," 179 pp., 1922.
16. Motry, Rev. Hubert Louis, S. T. D., J. C. D., Diocesan Faculties According to the Code of Canon Law, II-167 pp., 1922.
17. Murphy, Rev. George Lawrence, J. C. D., Delinquencies and Penalties in the Administration and the Reception of the Sacraments, IV-121 pp., 1923.

* All published numbers are available from the Catholic University of America Press, 620 Michigan Ave., N.E., Washington, D. C., except the following: nos. 1-114 inclusive, 116, 118, 120, 121, 122, 123, 136, 153, 162, 182 and 198. But the following numbers, now reissued, are obtainable from *The Jurist*, The Catholic University of America, Washington 17, D. C., namely: nos. 5, 7, 11, 17, 18, 19, 26, 28, 30, 31, 34, 42, 44, 51, 52 and 61.

18. O'Reilly, Rev. John Anthony, S. T. B., J. C. D., Ecclesiastical Sepulture in the New Code of Canon Law, II-129 pp., 1923.
19. Michalicka, Rev. Wenceslas Cyrill, O. S. B., J. C. D., Judicial Procedure in Dismissal of Clerical Exempt Religious, 107 pp., 1923.
20. Dargin, Rev. Edward Vincent, S. T. B., J. C. D., Reserved Cases According to the Code of Canon Law, IV-103 pp., 1924.
21. Godfrey, Rev. John A., S. T. B., J. C. D., The Right of Patronage According to the Code of Canon Law, 153 pp., 1924.
22. Hagerdon, Rev. Rev. Francis Edward, J. C. D., General Legislation on Indulgences, II-154 pp., 1924.
23. King, Rev. James Ignatius, J. C. D., The Administration of the Sacraments to Dying Non-Catholics, V-141 pp., 1924.
24. Winslow, Rev. Francis Joseph, O. F. M., J. C. D., Vicars and Prefects Apostolic, IV-149 pp., 1924.
25. Correa, Rev. Jose Servelion, S. T. L., J. C. D., La Potestad Legislativa de la Iglesia Catolica, IV-127 pp., 1925.
26. Dugan, Rev. Henry Francis, A. M., J. C. D., The Judiciary Department of the Diocesan Curia, 87 pp., 1925.
27. Keller, Rev. Charles Frederick, S. T. B., J. C. D., Mass Stipends, 167 pp., 1925.
28. Paschang, Rev. John Linus, J. C. D., The Sacramentals According to the Code of Canon Law, 129 pp., 1925.
29. Piontek, Rev. Cyrillus, O. F. M., S. T. B., J. C. D., De Indulto Exclaustrationis necnon Saecularizationis, XIII-289 pp., 1925.
30. Kearney, Rev. Richard Joseph, S. T. B., J. C. D., Sponsors at Baptism According to the Code of Canon Law, IV-127 pp., 1925.
31. Bartlett, Rev. Chester Joseph, A. M., LL. B., J. C D.., The Tenure of Parochial Property in the United States of America, V-108 pp., 1926.
32. Kilker, Rev. Adrian Jerome, J. C. D., Extreme Unction, V-425 pp., 1926.
33. Mc Cormick, Rev. Robert Emmett, J. C. D., Confessors of Religious, VIII-266 pp., 1926.
34. Miller, Rev. Newton Thomas, J. C. D., Founded Masses According to the Code of Canon Law, VII-93 pp., 1926.
35. Roelker, Rev. Edward G., S. T. D., J. C. D., Principles of Privilege According to the Code of Canon Law, XI-166 pp., 1926.
36. Bakalarczyk, Rev. Richardus, M. I. C., J. U. D., De Novitiatu, VIII-208 pp., 1927.
37. Pizzuti, Rev. Lawrence, O. F. M., J. U. L., De Parochis Religiosis, 1927, (Not Printed.)
38. Bliley, Rev. Nicholas Martin, O. S. B., J. C. D., Altars According to the Code of Canon Law, XIX-132 pp., 1927.
39. Brown, Mr. Brendan Francis, A. B., LL. M., J. U. D., The Canonical Juristic Personality with Special References to its Status in the United States of America, V-212 pp., 1927.

40. Cavanaugh, Rev. William Thomas, C. P., J. U. D., The Reservation of the Blessed Sacrament, VIII-101 pp., 1927.

41. Doheny, Rev. William J., C. S. C., A. B., J. U. D., Church Property: Modes of Acquisition, X-118 pp., 1927.

42. Feldhaus, Rev. Aloysius H., C. PP. S., J. C. D., Oratories, IX-141 pp., 1927.

43. Kelly, Rev. James Patrick, A. B., J. C. D., The Jurisdiction of the Simple Confessor, X-208 pp., 1927.

44. Neuberger, Rev. Nicholas J., J. C. D., Canon 6 or the Relation of the Codex Juris Canonici to the Preceding Legislation, V-95 pp., 1927.

45. O'Keefe, Rev. Gerald Michael, J. C. D., Matrimonial Dispensations, Powers of Bishops, Priests, and Confessors, VIII-232 pp., 1927.

46. Quigley, Rev. Joseph A. M., A. B., J. C. D., Condemned Societies, 139 pp., 1927.

47. Zaplotnik, Rev. Johannes Leo, J. C. D., De Vicariis Foraneis, X-142 pp., 1927.

48. Duskie, Rev. John Aloysius, A. B., J. C. D., The Canonical Status of the Orientals in the United States, VIII-196 pp., 1928.

49. Hyland, Rev. Francis Edward, J. C. D., Excommunication, Its Nature, Historical Development and Effects, VIII-181 pp., 1928.

50. Reinmann, Rev. Gerald Joseph, O. M. C., J. C. D., The Third Order Secular of Saint Francis, 201 pp., 1928.

51. Schenk, Rev. Francis J., J. C. D., The Matrimonial Impediments of Mixed Religion and Disparity of Cult, XVI-318 pp., 1929.

52. Coady, Rev. John Joseph, S. T. D., J. U. D., A. M., The Appointment of Pastors, VIII-150 pp., 1929.

53. Kay, Rev. Thomas Henry, J. C. D., Competence in Matrimonial Procedure, VIII-164 pp., 1929.

54. Turner, Rev. Sidney Joseph, C. P., J. U. D., The Vow of Poverty, XLIX-217 pp., 1929.

55. Kearney, Rev. Raymond A., A. B., S. T. D., J. C. D., The Principles of Delegation, VII-149 pp., 1929.

56. Conran, Rev. Edward James, A. B., J. C. D., The Interdict, V-163 pp., 1930.

57. O'Neill, Rev. William H., J. C. D., Papal Rescripts of Favor, VII-218 pp., 1930.

58. Bastnagel, Rev. Clement Vincent, J. U. D., The Appointment of Parochial Adjutants and Assistants, XV-257 pp., 1930.

59. Ferry, Rev. William A., A. B., J. C. D., Stole Fees, V-136 pp., 1930.

60. Costello, Rev. John Michael, A. B., J. C. D., Domicile and Quasi-Domicile, VII-201 pp., 1930.

61. Kremer, Rev. Michael Nicholas, A. B., S. T. B., J. C. D., Church Support in the United States, VI-136 pp., 1930.

62. Angulo, Rev. Luis, C. M., J. C. D., Legislacion de la Iglesia sobre la intencion en la aplicacion de la Santa Misa, VII-104 pp., 1931.

63. Frey, Rev. Wolfgang Norbert, O. S. B., A. B., J. C. D., The Act of Religious Profession, VIII-174 pp., 1931.

64. Roberts, Rev. James Brendan, A. B., J. C. D., The Banns of Marriage, XIV-140 pp., 1931.
65. Ryder, Rev. Raymond Aloysius, A. B., J. C. D., Simony, IX-151 pp., 1931.
66. Campagna, Rev. Angelo, Ph. D., J. U. D., Il Vicario Generale del Vescovo, VII-205 pp., 1931.
67. Cox, Rev. Joseph Godfrey, A. B., J. C. D., The Administration of Seminaries, VI-124 pp., 1931.
68. Gregory, Rev. Donald J., J. U. D., The Pauline Privilege, XV-165 pp., 1931.
69. Donohue, Rev. John F., J. C. D., The Impediment of Crime, VII-110 pp., 1931.
70. Dooley, Rev. Eugene A., O. M. I., J. C. D., Church Law on Sacred Relics, IX-143 pp., 1931.
71. Orth, Rev. Clement Raymond, O. M. C., J. C. D., The Approbation of Religious Institutes, 171 pp., 1931.
72. Pernicone, Rev. Joseph M., A. B., J. C. D., The Ecclesiastical Prohibition of Books, XII-267 pp., 1932.
73. Clinton, Rev. Connell, A. B., J. C. D., The Paschal Precept, IX-108 pp., 1932.
74. Donnelly, Rev. Francis B., A. M., S. T. L., J. C. D., The Diocesan Synod, VIII-125 pp., 1932.
75. Torrente, Rev. Camilo, C. M. F., J. C. D., Las Procesiones Sagradas, V-145 pp., 1932.
76. Murphy, Rev. Edwin J., C. PP. S., J. C. D., Suspension Ex Informata Conscientia, XI-122 pp., 1932.
77. MacKenzie, Rev. Eric F., A. M., S. T. L., J. C. D., The Delict of Heresy in its Commission, Penalization, Absolution, VII-124 pp., 1932.
78. Lyons, Rev. Avitus E., S. T. B., J. C. D., The Collegiate Tribunal of First Instance, XI-147 pp., 1932.
79. Connolly, Rev. Thomas A., J. C. D., Appeals, XI-195 pp., 1932.
80. Sangmeister, Rev. Joseph V., A. B., J. C. D., Force and Fear as Precluding Matrimonial Consent, V-211 pp., 1932.
81. Jaeger, Rev. Leo A., A. B., J. C. D., The Administration of Vacant and Quasi-Vacant Episcopal Sees in the United States, IX-229 pp., 1932.
82. Rimlinger, Rev. Herbert T., J. C. D., Error Invalidating Matrimonial Consent, VII-79 pp., 1932.
83. Barrett, Rev. John D. M., SS., J. C. D., A Comparative Study of the Councils of Baltimore and the Code of Canon Law, X-223 pp., 1932.
84. Carberry, Rev. John J., Ph. D., S. T. D., J.C.D., The Juridicial Form of Marriage, X-177 pp., 1934.
85. Dolan, Rev. John L., A. B., J. C. D., The Defensor Vinculi, XII-157 pp., 1934.
86. Hannan, Rev. Jerome D., A. M., S. T. D., LL. B., J. C. D., The Canon Law of Wills, IX-517 pp., 1934.
87. Lemieux, Rev. Delise A., A. M., J. C. D., The Sentence in Ecclesiastical Procedure, IX-131 pp., 1934.

88. O'Rourke, Rev. James J., A. B., J. C. D., Parish Registers, VII-109 pp., 1934.
89. Timlin, Rev. Bartholomew, O. F. M., A. M., J. C. D., Conditional Matrimonial Consent, X-381 pp., 1934.
90. Wahl, Rev. Francis X., A. B., J. C. D., The Matrimonial Impediments of Consanguinity and Affinity, VI-125 pp., 1934.
91. White, Rev. Robert J., A. B., LL. B., S. T. B., J. C. D., Canonical Ante-Nuptial Promises and the Civil Law, VI-152 pp., 1934.
92. Herrera, Rev. Antonio Parra, O. C. D., J. C. D., Legislacion Eclesiastica sobra el Ayuno y la Abstinencia, XI-191 pp., 1935.
93. Kennedy, Rev. Edwin J., J. C. D., The Special Matrimonial Process in Cases of Evident Nullity, X-165 pp., 1935.
94. Manning, Rev. John J., A. B., J. C. D., Presumption of Law in Matrimonial Procedure, XI-111 pp., 1935.
95. Moeder, Rev. John M., J. C. D., The Proper Bishop for Ordination and Dismissorial Letters, VII-135 pp., 1935.
96. O'Mara, Rev. William A., A. B., J. C. D., Canonical Causes for Matrimonial Dispensations, IX-155 pp., 1935.
97. Reilly, Rev. Peter, J. C. D., Residence of Pastors, IX-81 pp., 1935.
98. Smith, Rev. Mariner T., O. P., S. T. Lr., J. C. D., The Penal Law for Religious, VII-169 pp., 1935.
99. Whalen, Rev. Donald W., A. M., J. C. D., The Value of Testimonial Evidence in Matrimonial Procedure, XIII-297 pp., 1935.
100. Cleary, Rev. Joseph F., J. C. D., Canonical Limitations on the Alienation of Church Property, VIII-141 pp., 1936.
101. Glynn, Rev. John C., J. C. D., The Promoter of Justice, XX-337 pp., 1936.
102. Brennan, Rev. James H., S. S., M. A., S. T. B., J. C. D., The Simple Convalidation of Marriage, VI-135 pp., 1937.
103. Brunini, Rev. Joseph Bernard, J. C. D., The Clerical Obligations of Canons 139 and 142, X-121 pp., 1937.
104. Connor, Rev. Maurice, A. B., J. C. D., The Administrative Removal of Pastors, VIII-159 pp., 1937.
105. Guilfoyle, Rev. Merlin Joseph, J. C. D., Custom, XI-144 pp., 1937.
106. Hughes, Rev. James Austin, A. B., A. M., J. C. D., Witnesses in Criminal Trials of Clerics, IX-140 pp., 1937.
107. Jansen, Rev. Raymond J., A. B., S. T. L., J. C. D., Canonical Provisions for Catechetical Instruction, VII-153 pp., 1937.
108. Kealy, Rev. John James, A. B., J. C. D., The Introductory Libellus in Church Court Procedure, XI-121 pp., 1937.
109. McManus, Rev. James Edward, C. SS. R., J. C. D., The Administration of Temporal Goods in Religious Institutes, XVI-196 pp., 1937.
110. Moriarty, Rev. Eugene James, J. C. D., Oaths in Ecclesiastical Courts, X-115 pp., 1937.
111. Rainer, Rev. Eligius George, C. SS. R., J. C. D., Suspension of Clerics, XVII-249 pp., 1937.

112. Reilly, Rev. Thomas F., C. SS. R., J. C. D., Visitation of Religious, VI-195 pp., 1938.
113. Moriarty, Rev. Francis E., C. SS. R., J. C. D., The Extraordinary Absolution from Censures, XV-334 pp., 1938.
114. Connolly, Rev. Nicholas P., J. C. D., The Canonical Erection of Parishes, X-132 pp., 1938.
115. Donovan, Rev. James Joseph, J. C. D., The Pastor's Obligation in Prenuptial Investigation, XII-322 pp., 1938.
116. Harrigan, Rev. Robert J., M. A., S. T. B., J. C. D., The Radical Sanation of Invalid Marriages, VIII-208 pp., 1938.
117. Boffa, Rev. Conrad Humbert, J. C. D., Canonical Provisions for Catholic Schools, VII-211 pp., 1939.
118. Parsons, Rev. Anscar John, O. M. Cap., J. C. D., Canonical Elections, XII-236 pp., 1939.
119. Reilly, Rev. Edward Michael, A. B., J. C. D., The General Norms of Dispensation, XII-156 pp., 1939.
120. Ryan, Rev. Gerald Aloysius, A. B., J. C. D., Principles of Episcopal Jurisdiction, XII-172 pp., 1939.
121. Burton, Rev. Francis James, C. S. C., A. B., J. C. D., A Commentary on Canon 1125, X-222 pp., 1940.
122. Miaskiewicz, Rev. Francis Sigismund, J. C. D., Supplied Jurisdiction According to Canon 209, XII-340 pp., 1940.
123. Rice, Rev. Patrick William, A. B., J. C. D., Proof of Death in Prenuptial Investigation, VII-156 pp., 1940.
124. Anglin, Rev. Thomas Francis, M. S., J. C D., T.he Eucharist Fast, VIII-183 pp., 1941.
125. Coleman, Rev. John Jerome, J. C. D., The Minister of Confirmation, VI-153 pp. 1941.
126. Downs, Rev. John Emmanuel, A. B., J. C. D., The Concept of Clerical Immunity, XI-163 pp., 1941.
127. Esswein, Rev. Anthony Albert, J. C. D., Extrajudicial Penal Powers of Ecclesiastical Superiors, X-144 pp., 1941.
128. Farrell, Rev. Benjamin Francis, M. A., S. T. L., J. C. D., The Rights and Duties of the Local Ordinary Regarding Congregations of Women Religious of Pontifical Approval, V-195 pp., 1941.
129. Feeney, Rev. Thomas John, A. B., S. T. L., J. C. D., Restitutio in Integrum, VI-169 pp., 1941.
130. Findlay, Rev. Stephen William, O. S. B., A .B., J. C. D., Canonical Norms Governing the Deposition and Degredation of Clerics, XVII-279 pp., 1941.
131. Goodwine, Rev. John, A. B., S. T. L., J. C. D., The Right of the Church to Acquire Property, VIII-119 pp., 1941.
132. Heston, Rev. Edward Louis, C. S. C., Ph. D., S. T. D., J. C. D., The Alienation of Church Property in the United States, XII-222 pp., 1941.
133. Hogan, Rev. James John, A. B., S. T. L., J. C. D., Judicial Advocates and Procurators, XIII-200 pp., 1941.

134. KEALY, REV. THOMAS M., A. B., LITT. B., J. C. D., Dowry of Women Re-gious, IX-152 pp., 1941.
135. KEENE, REV. MICHAEL JAMES, O. S. B., J. C. D., Religious Ordinaries and Canon 198, V-164 pp., 1941 (Printed 1942).
136. KERIN, REV. CHARLES A., S. S., M .A., S. T. B., J. C. D., The Privation of Christian Burial, XVI-279 pp., 1941.
137. LOUIS, REV. WILLIAM FRANCIS, M. A., J. C. D., Diocesan Archives, X-101 pp., 1941.
138. MCDEVITT, REV. GILBERT JOSEPH, A. B., J. C. D., Legitimacy and Legitimation, X-247 pp., 1941.
139. MCDONOUGH, REV. THOMAS JOSEPH, A. B., J. C. D., Apostolic Administrators, X-217 pp., 1941.
140. MEIER, REV. CARL ANTHONY, A. B., J. C. D., Penal Administrative Procedure Against Negligent Pastors, XI-240 pp., 1941.
141. SCHMIDT, REV. JOHN ROGG, A. B., J. C. D., The Principles of Authentic Interpretation in Canon 17 of the Code of Canon Law, XII-331 pp., 1941.
142. SLAFKOSKY, REV. ANDREW LEONARD, A. B., J. C. D., The Canonical Episcopal Visitation of the Diocese, X-197 pp., 1941.
143. SWOBODA, REV. INNOCENT ROBERT, O. F. M., J. C. D., Ignorance in Relation to the Imputability of Delicts, IX-271 pp., 1941.
144. DUBE, REV. ARTHUR JOSEPH, A. B., J. C. D., The General Principles for the Reckoning of Time in Canon Law, VIII-299 pp., 1941.
145. MCBRIDE, REV. JAMES T., A. B., J. C. D., Incardination and Excardination of Seculars, XX-585 pp., 1941.
146. KROL, REV. JOHN T., J. C. D., The Defendant in Ecclesiastical Trials, XII-207 pp., 1942.
147. COMYNS, REV. JOSEPH J., C. SS. R., A. B., J. C. D., Papal and Episcopal Administration of Church Property, XIV-155 pp., 1942.
148. BARRY, REV. GARRETT FRANCIS, O. M. I., J. C. D., Violation of the Cloister, XII-260 pp., 1942.
149. BOLDUC, REV. GATIEN, C. S. V., A. B., S. T. L., J. C. D., Les Etudes dans les Religions Clericales, VIII-155 pp., 1942.
150. BOYLE, REV. DAVID JOHN, M. A., J. C. D., The Juridic Effects of Moral Certitude on Pre-Nuptial Guarantees, XII-188 pp., 1942.
151. CANAVAN, REV. WALTER JOSEPH, M. A., LITT. D., J. C. D., The Profession of Faith, XII-143 pp., 1942.
152. DESROCHERS, REV. BRUNO, A. B., PH. L., S. T. B., J. C. D., Le Premier Concile Plenier de Quebec et le Code de Droit Canonique, XIV-186 pp., 1942.
153. DILLON, REV. ROBERT EDWARD, A. B., J. C. D., Common Law Marriage, X-148 pp., 1942.
154. DODWELL, REV. EDWARD JOHN, PH. D., S. T. B., J. C. D., The Time and Place for the Celebration of Marriage, X-156 pp., 1942.
155. DONNELLAN, REV. THOMAS ANDREW, A. B., J. C. D., The Obligation of the Missa pro Populo, VII-131 pp., 1942.

156. Eltz, Rev. Louis Anthony, A. B., J. C. D., Cooperation in Crime, XII-208 pp., 1942.
157. Gass, Rev. Sylvester Francis, M. A., J. C. D., Ecclesiastical Pensions, XI-206 pp., 1942.
158. Guiniven, Rev. John Joseph, C. SS. R., J. C. D., The Precept of Hearing Mass, XIV-199 pp., 1942.
159. Gulczynski, Rev. John Theophilus, J. C. D., The Desecration and Violation of Churches, X-126 pp., 1942.
160. Hammill, Rev. John Leo, M. A., J. C. D., The Obligations of the Traveler According to Canon 14, VII-204 pp., 1942.
161. Haydt, Rev. John Joseph, A. B., J. C. D., Reserved Benefices, XI-148 pp., 1942.
162. Huser, Rev. Roger John, O. F. M., A. B., J. C. D., The Crime of Abortion in Canon Law, XII-187 pp., 1942.
163. Kearney, Rev. Francis Patrick, A. B., S. T. L., J. C. D., The Principles of Canon 1127, X-162 pp., 1942.
164. Linahen, Rev. Leo James, S. T. L., J. C. D., De Absolutione Complicis in Peccato Turpi, V-114 pp., 1942.
165. McCloskey, Rev. Joseph Aloysius, A. B., J. C. D., The Subject of Ecclesiastical Law According to Canon 12, XVII-246 pp., 1942 (Printed 1943).
166. O'Neill, Rev. Francis Joseph, C. SS. R., J. C. D., The Dismissal of Religious in Temporary Vows, VIII-220 pp., 1942.
167. Prince, Rev. John Edward, A. B., S. T. B., J. C. D., The Diocesan Chancellor, X-136 pp., 1942.
168. Riesner, Rev. Albert Joseph, C. SS. R., J. C. D., Apostates and Fugitives from Religious Institutes, IX-168 pp., 1942.
169. Stenger, Rev. Joseph Bernard, J. C. D., The Mortgaging of Church Property, 186 pp., 1942.
170. Waldron, Rev. Joseph Francis, A. B., J. C. D., The Minister of Baptism, XII-197 pp., 1942.
171. Willett, Rev. Robert Albert, J. C. D., The Probative Value of Documents in Ecclesiastical Trials, X-124 pp., 1942.
172. Woeber, Rev. Edward Martin, M. A., J. C. D., The Interpellations, XII-161 pp., 1942.
173. Benko, Rev. Matthew Aloysius, O. S. B., M. A., J. C. D., The Abbot *Nullius*, XVI-148 pp., 1943.
174. Christ, Rev. Joseph James, M. A., S. T. L., J. C. D., Dispensation from Vindicative Penalties, XIV-285 pp., 1943.
175. Clancy, Rev. Patrick M. J., O. P., A. B., S. T. Lr., J. C. D., The Local Religious Superior, X-229 pp., 1943.
176. Clarke, Rev. Thomas James, J.C.D., Parish Societies, XII-147 pp., 1943.
177. Connolly, Rev. John Patrick, S. T. L., J. C. D., Synodal Examiners and Parish Priest Consultors, X-223 pp., 1943.
178. Drumm, Rev. William Martin, A. B., J. C. D., Hospital Chaplains, XII-175 pp., 1943.

179. Flanagan, Rev. Bernard Joseph, A. B., S. T. L., J. C. D., The Canonical Erection of Religious Houses, X-147 pp., 1943.

180. Kelleher, Rev. Stephen Joseph, A. B., S. T. B., J. C. D., Discussions with Non-Catholics: Canonical Legislation, X-93 pp., 1943.

181. Lewis, Rev. Gordian, C. P., J. C. D., Chapters in Religious Institutes, XII-169 pp., 1943.

182. Marx, Rev. Adolph, J. C. D., The Declaration of Nullity of Marriages Contracted Outside the Church, X-151 pp., 1943.

183. Matulenas, Rev. Raymond Anthony, O. S. B., A. B., J. C. D., Communication, a Source of Privileges, XII-225 pp., 1943.

184. O'Leary, Rev. Charles Gerard, C. SS. R., J. C. D., Religious Dismissed After Perpetual Profession, X-213 pp., 1943.

185. Power, Rev. Cornelius Michael, J. C. D., The Blessing of Cemeteries, XII-231 pp., 1943.

186. Shuhler, Rev. Ralph Vincent, O. S. A., J. C. D., Privileges of Religious to Absolve and Dispense, XII-195 pp., 1943.

187. Ziolkowski, Rev. Thaddeus Stanislaus, A. B., J. C. D., The Consecration and Blessing of Churches, XII-151 pp., 1943.

188. Heneghan, Rev. John Joseph, S. T. D., The Marriages of Unworthy Catholics: Canons 1065 and 1066, XVI-213 pp., 1944.

189. Carroll, Rev. Coleman Francis, M. A., S. T. L., J. C. L., Charitable Institutions.

190. Ciesluk, Rev. Joseph Edward, Ph. B., S. T. L., J. C. D., National Parishes in the United States, VI-178 pp., 1944.

191. Coburn, Rev. Vincent Paul, A. B., J. C. D., Marriages of Conscience, XII-172 pp., 1944.

192. Connors, Rev. Charles Paul, C. S. Sp., A. B., J. C. D., Extra-Judicial Procurators in the Code of Canon Law, X-94 pp., 1944.

193. Coyle, Rev. Paul Raymond, A. B., J. C. D., Judicial Exceptions, X-142 pp., 1944.

194. Fair. Rev. Bartholomew Francis, A. B., S. T. L., J. C. D., The Impediment of Abduction, XII-122 pp., 1944.

195. Gallagher, Rev. Thomas Raphael, O. P., A. B., S. T. Lr., J. C. D., The Examination of the Qualities of the Ordinand, X-166 pp., 1944.

196. Gannon, Rev. John Mark, S. T. L., J. C. D., The Interstices Required for the Promotion to Orders, XII-100 pp., 1944.

197. Goldsmith, Rev. J. William, B. C. S., S. T. L., J. C. D., The Competence of Church and State Over Marriages—Disputed Points, X-128 pp., 1944.

198. Goodwine, Rev. Joseph Gerard, A. B., S. T. B., J. C. D., The Reception of Converts, XIV-326 pp., 1944.

199. Kowalski, Rev. Romuald Eugene, O. F. M., A. B., J. C. D., Sustenance of Religious Houses of Regulars, X-174 pp., 1944.

200. McCoy, Rev. Alan Edward, O. F. M., J. C. D., Force and Fear in Relation to Delictual Imputability and Penal Responsibility, XII-160 pp., 1944.

201. McDevitt, Rev. Vincent John, Ph. B., S. T. L., J. C. L., Perjury.

202. Martin, Rev. Thomas Owen, Ph. D., S. T. D., J. C. D., Adverse Possession, Prescription and Limitation of Actions: The Canonical "Praescriptio," XX-208 pp., 1944.

203. Miklosovic, Rev. Paul John, A. B., J. C. L., Attempted Marriages and Their Consequent Juridic Effects.

204. Mundy, Rev. Thomas Maurice, A. B., S. T. L., J. C. D., The Union of Parishes, X-164 pp., 1944.

205. O'Dea, Rev. John Coyle, A. B., J. C. D., The Matrimonial Impediment of Nonage, VIII-126 pp., 1944.

206. Olalia, Rev. Alexander Ayson, S. T. L., J. C. D., A Comparative Study of the Christian Constitution of States and the Constitution of the Philippine Commonwealth, XII-136 pp., 1944.

207. Poisson, Rev. Pierre-Marie, C. S. C., A. B., Ph. L., Th. L., J. C. L., Droits Patrimoniaux des Maisons et des Eglises Religieuses.

208. Stadalnikas, Rev. Casimir Joseph, M. I. C., J. C. D., Reservation of Censures, X-141 pp., 1944.

209. Sullivan, Rev. Eugene Henry, S. T. L., J. C. D., Proof of the Reception of the Sacraments, X-165 pp., 1944.

210. Vaughan, Rev. William Edward, J. C. D., Constitutions for Diocesan Courts, X-210 pp., 1944.

211. Paro, Rev. Gino, S. T. D., J. C. D., The Right of Papal Legation, X-221 pp., 1947.

212. Balzer, Rev. Ralph Francis, C. P., J. C. D., The Computation of Time in a Canonical Novitiate, X-227 pp., 1945.

213. Dougherty, Rev. John Whelan, A. B., S. T. L., J. C. D., De Inquisitione Speciali, XII-195 pp., 1945.

214. Dziob, Rev. Michael Walter, J. C. D., The Sacred Congregation for the Oriental Church, XII-181 pp., 1945.

215. Eidenschink, Rev. John Albert, O. S. B., B. A., J. C. D., The Election of Bishops in the Letters of Pope Gregory the Great, VII-200 pp., 1945.

216. Gill, Rev. Nicholas, C. P., J. C. D., The Spiritual Prefect in Clerical Religious Houses of Study, X-140 pp., 1945.

217. Hynes, Rev. Harry Gerard, S. T. L., J. C. D., The Privileges of Cardinals, XII-183 pp., 1945.

218. McDevitt, Rev. Gerald Vincent, S. T. L., J. C. D., The Renunciation of an Ecclesiastical Office, XIV-179 pp., 1945.

219. Manning, Rev. Joseph Leroy, J. C. D., The Free Conferral of Offices, VII-116 pp., 1945.

220. Meyer, Rev. Louis G., O. S. B., A. B., S. T. B., J. C. D., Alms-gathering by Religious, XII-163 pp., 1945.

221. O'Donnell, Rev. Cletus Francis, M. A., J. C. D., The Marriage of Minors, XII-268 pp., 1945.

222. Prunskis, Rev. Joseph, J. C. D., Comparative Law, Ecclesiastical and Civil, in Lithuanian Concordat, X-161 pp., 1945.

223. Sweeney, Rev. Francis Patrick, C. SS. R., J. C. D., The Reduction of Clerics to the Lay State, X-199 pp., 1945.
224. Vogelpohl, Rev. Henry John, J. C. D., The Simple Impediments to Holy Orders, XVI-190 pp., 1945.
225. Brockhaus, Rev. Thomas Aquinas, O. S. B., J. C. D., Religious Who Are Known as *Conversi*, X-127 pp., 1945.
226. Griese, Rev. Orville Nicholas, S. T. D., J. C. D., Marriage and the Procreation of Offspring, XVI-224 pp., 1945.
227. Boudreaux, Rev. Warren Louis, J. C. D., The "*ab acatholicis nati*" of Canon 1099, § 2, XII-110 pp., 1946.
228. Bowe, Rev. Thomas Joseph, A. B., J. C. D., Religious Superioresses, VIII-206 pp., 1946.
229. Diederichs, Rev. Michael Ferdinand, S. C. J., J. C. D., The Jurisdiction of the Latin Ordinaries over their Oriental Subjects, XIV-153 pp., 1946.
230. Dingman, Rev. Maurice John, A. B., S. T. L., J. C. L., The Plaintiff in Contentious Trials.
231. Frison, Rev. Basil, C. M. F., M. Mus., J. C. D., The Retroactivity of Law, X-221 pp., 1946.
232. Galvin, Rev. William Anthony, M. A., J. C. D., The Administrative Transfer of Pastors, XII-288 pp., 1946.
233. Goracy, Rev. Joseph C., J. C. L., The Diriment of Matrimonial Impediment of Major Orders.
234. Hale, Rev. Joseph Francis, M. A., S. T. L., J. C. D., The Pastor of Burial, X-247 pp., 1946 (Printed 1949).
235. Henry, Rev. Joseph Arthur, A. B., J. C. D., The Mass and Holy Communion: Interritual Law, XII-138 pp., 1946.
236. Linenberger, Rev. Herbert, C. PP. S., J. C. D., The False Denunciation of an Innocent Confessor, VIII-205 pp., 1946 (Printed 1949).
237. Lowry, Rev. James Martin, A. B., J. C. D., Dispensation from Private Vows, XII-216 pp., 1946.
238. Lynch, Rev. George Edward, A. B., S. T. L., J. C. D., Coadjutors and Auxiliaries of Bishops, X-107 pp., 1946 (Printed 1947).
239. Lynch, Rev. Timothy, M. S. SS. T., J. C. D., Contracts between Bishops and Religious Congregations, XIII-232 pp., 1946.
240. McClunn, Rev. Justin David, A. B., S. T. L., J. C. D., Administrative Recourse, VII-142 pp., 1946.
241. Lohmuller, Rev. Martin Nicholas, A. B., J. C. D., The Promulgation of Law, XII-140 pp., 1947.
242. McGrath, Rev. James, A. B., J. C. D., The Privilege of the Canon, XII-156 pp., 1946.
243. Marbach, Rev. Joseph Francis, A. B., J. C. D., Marriage Legislation for the Catholics of the Oriental Rites in the United States and Canada, XIV-314 pp., 1946.
244. Shimkus, Rev. Bernard Aloysius, A. B., J. C. L., The Determination and Transfer of Rite.

245. SMITH, REV. VINCENT MICHAEL, A. B., S. T. L., J. C. L., Ignorance Affecting Matrimonial Consent.

246. WACHTRLE, REV. PAUL ANTHONY, A. B., J. C. L., The Baptism of the Children of Non-Catholics.

247. CROTTY, REV. MATTHEW M., J. C. D., The Recipient of First Holy Communion, X-142 pp., 1947.

248. EAGLETON, REV. GEORGE, J. C. D., The Quinquennial Faculties, Formula IV, XIV-199 pp., 1947 (Printed 1948).

249. GIBBONS, REV. MARION L., C. M., LL. B., J. C. D., Domicile of the Wife Unlawfully Separated from Her Husband, XIV-171 pp., 1947.

250. KELLY, REV. BERNARD M., S. T. L., J. C. D., The Functions Reserved to Pastors, IX-141 pp., 1947.

251. KILCULLEN, REV. THOMAS J., LL. M., J. C. D., The Collegiate Moral Person as Party Litigant, X-150 pp., 1947.

252. LAFONTAINE, REV. GERMAIN J., W. F., J. C. D., Relations Canoniques entre Le Missionnaire et Ses Superieurs, X-117 pp., 1947.

253. LANE, REV. LORAS T., A. B., S. T. L., J. C. D., Matrimonial Procedure in the Ordinary Court of Second Instance, XVI-184 pp., 1947.

254. LOVER, REV. JAMES F., C. SS. R., J. C. D., The Master of Novices, X-168 pp., 1947.

255. McNICHOLAS, REV. TIMOTHY J., J. C. L., The *Septimae Manus* Witness.

256. MAROSITZ, REV. JOSEPH J., M. S. C., J. C. D., Obligations and Privileges of Religious Promoted to the Episcopal or Cardinalitial Dignities, XII-180 pp., 1947.

257. MURPHY, REV. FRANCIS J., A. B., J. C. D., Legislative Powers of the Provincial Council, XII-158 pp., 1947.

258. O'BRIEN, REV. ROMAEUS W., O. CARM., J. C. D., The Provincial Superior in Religious Orders of Men, X-294 pp., 1947.

259. PFALLER, REV. BENEDICT A., O. S. B., J. C. D., The *Ipso facto* Effected Dismissal of Religious, XII-225 pp., 1947.

260. POPEK, REV. ALPHONSE S., M. A., J. C. D., The Rights and Obligations of Metropolitans, XX-460 pp., 1947.

261. RISTUCCIA, REV. BERNARD J., C. M., J. C. D., Quasi-Religious, XVI-318 pp., 1947 (Printed 1949).

262. SONNTAG, REV. NATHANIEL L., O. F. M. CAP., J. C. D., Censorship of Special Classes of Books, XII-147 pp., 1947.

263. STADLER, REV. JOSEPH N., J. C. D., Frequent Holy Communion, X-158 pp., 1947.

264. SZAL, REV. IGNATIUS J., J. C. D., The Communication of Catholics with Schismatics, XII-217 pp., 1947.

265. WAGNER, REV. URBAN S., O. F. M. CONV., J. C. D., Parochial Substitute Vicars and Supplying Priests, IX-126 pp., 1947.

266. QUINN, REV. JOSEPH, M. A., J. C. D., Documents Required for the Reception of Orders, XII-207 pp., 1948.

267. Bennington, Rev. James Clement, A. B., J. C. L., The Recipient of Confirmation.

268. Blaher, Rev. Damian Joseph, O. F. M., A. B., J. C. L., The Ordinary Processes in Causes of Beatification and Canonization.

269. Clune, Rev. Robert Bell, B. A., J. C. L., The Judicial Interrogation of the Parties.

270. Courtemanche, Rev. Basil F., B. A., J. C. L., The Total Simulation of Matrimonial Consent.

271. Dlouhy, Rev. Maur John, O. S. B., A. B., J. C. L., The Ordination of Exempt Religious.

272. Donovan, Rev. John Thomas, Ph. B., S. T. L., J. C. D., The Clerical Obligations of Canons 138 and 140, XII-209 pp., 1948.

273. Freking, Rev. Frederick W., A. B., S. T. B., J. C. L., The Canonical Installation of Pastors.

274. Fulton, Rev. Thomas B., J. C. L., Prenuptial Investigation.

275. Godley, Rev. James P., J. C. L., The Time and the Place for the Celebration of Mass.

276. Kane, Rev. Thomas A., A. B., B. S., J. C. D., The Jurisdiction of the Patriarchs of the Major Sees in Antiquity and in the Middle Ages, XII-111 pp., 1948 (Printed 1949).

277. Kennedy, Rev. Andrew A., J. C. L., The Annual Pastoral Report to the Local Ordinary.

278. Konrad, Rev. Joseph George, J. C. L., Transfer of Religious.

279. Kress, Rev. Alphonse, J. C. L., Contumacy in Ecclesiastical Trials.

280. McCartney, Rev. Marcellus Anthony, O. F. M., M. A., J. C. L., Faculties of Regular Confessors.

281. McCaslin, Rev. Edward Patrick, M. A., S. T. L., J. C. L., The Division of Parishes.

282. McElroy, Rev. Francis J., A. B., J. C. L., The Privileges of Bishops.

283. Quinn, Rev. Stephen, M. S. SS. T., J. C. D., Relation between the Local Ordinary and Religious of Diocesan Approval, XII-153 pp., 1948 (Printed 1949).

284. Schneider, Rev. Edelhard Louis, A. D. S., M. A., J. C. D., The Status of Secularized Ex-Religious Clerics, X-155 pp., 1948.

285. Thompson, Rev. Chester J., A. B., J. C. L., The Simple Removal from Office.

286. O'Brien, Rev. Kenneth R., A. B., J. C. D., The Nature of Support of Diocesan Priests in the United States, XVI-162 pp., 1949.

287. Metz, Rev. John E., S. T. L., J. C. D., The Recording Judge in the Ecclesiastical Collegiate Tribunal, X-130 pp., 1949.

288. Reinhardt, Rev. Marion J., S. T. L., J. C. L., The Rogatory Commission.

289. Ortega Uhink, Rev. Juan, S. J., J. C. L., De Delicto Sollicitationis.

290. Casey, Rev. James V., J. C. L., A Study of Canon 2222, § 1.

291. Allgeier, Rev. Joseph L., J. C. L., The Canonical Obligation of Preaching in Parish Churches.

292. CAHILL, REV. DANIEL R., J. C. L., The Custody of the Holy Eucharist.
293. CARR, REV. AIDAN, O. F. M. CONV., S. T. D., J. C. L., Vocation to the Priesthood: Its Canonical Concept.
294. KNOPKE, REV. ROCH F., O. F. M., J. C. L., Reverential Fear in Matrimonial Cases in Asiatic Countries: Rota Cases.
295. LAVELLE, REV. HOWARD D., J. C. L., The Obligation of Holding Sacred Missions in Parishes.
296. MICHELLS, REV. ANTHONY B., J. C. L., The Constitutive Elements of Parishes.
297. NOONE, REV. JOHN J., J. C. L., Nullity in Judicial Acts.
298. SHEEHAN, REV. DANIEL E., J. C. L., The Minister of Holy Communion.
299. STATKUS, REV. FRANCIS J., J. C. L., The Minister of the Last Sacraments.
300. COOK, REV. JOHN P., J. C. L., Ecclesiastical Communities and Their Ability to Induce Legal Customs.
301. FAZZALARO, REV. FRANCIS J., J. C. L., The Place for the Hearing of Confessions.
302. HANNAN, REV. PHILIP M., J. C. L., The Canonical Concept of *congrua sustentatio* for the Secular Clergy.
303. QUINN, REV. HUGH G., J. C. L., The Particular Penal Precept.
304. GALLAGHER, REV. JOHN F., J. C. L., The Matrimonial Impediment of Public Propriety.
305. WELSH, REV. THOMAS J., J. C. L., The Use of the Portable Altar.